Workshop on Parsing German 2008

(PaGe 08)

Held in conjunction with ACL-HLT 2008

Columbus, Ohio, USA
20 June 2008

ISBN: 978-1-61738-553-7

Printed from e-media with permission by:

Curran Associates, Inc.
57 Morehouse Lane
Red Hook, NY 12571

Some format issues inherent in the e-media version may also appear in this print version.

Printed by Curran Associates, Inc. (2010)

For permission requests, please contact the Association for Computational Linguistics at the address below.

Association for Computational Linguistics
209 N. Eighth Street
Stroudsburg, Pennsylvania 18360

Phone: 1-570-476-8006
Fax: 1-570-476-0860

acl@aclweb.org

Additional copies of this publication are available from:

Curran Associates, Inc.
57 Morehouse Lane
Red Hook, NY 12571 USA
Phone: 845-758-0400
Fax: 845-758-2634
Email: curran@proceedings.com
Web: www.proceedings.com

Introduction

Welcome to the ACL Workshop on Parsing German, the first of what we hope will be a long and fruitful series of workshops on this topic.

German possesses an interesting set of configurational properties on the syntactic level which make it far less flexible with respect to word order than other free word order languages. Analyses of these properties, which have formed a part of the traditional syntax of German since the early 19th century, only re-entered the mainstream of generative linguistics research within the last twenty years or so. In computational linguistics, however, their realization has varied quite widely: "topological fields" in HPSG-style analyses, multiple parse trees, special constraints on liberation in constraint-based dependency-style analyses, various hybrid "deep/shallow" approaches, and agnostic parameter estimation over graphs. This variation can also acutely be felt in the annotation of German treebanks. Many corpora have historically elected to annotate only a few of the different senses of the term "constituent" inherent to German syntax, resulting in standards that make German appear either more like English or more like Czech.

The aim of this workshop was to provide a forum for theoretical discussion as well as a shared task, based on the TIGER and TueBa-D/Z German treebanks, for these various approaches to make their case on empirical grounds. This combination we believe to be essential to balancing the considerations of what structure merits learning versus the ease with which it can be learned. Both treebanks are annotated collections of German newspaper text on similar topics. They are annotated with POS, morphology, phrase structure, and grammatical functions. TueBa-D/Z additionally uses topological fields to describe fundamental word order restrictions in German clauses. The treebanks differ significantly in their annotation schemes, however: while TIGER relies on crossing branches to describe long distance relationships, TueBa-D/Z uses pure tree structures with designated labels for long distance relationships. Additionally, the annotation is TIGER is flat on the phrasal level while TueBa-D/Z annotates phrasal structure more hierarchically.

A report on the results of this year's shared task can be found in the final paper of these proceedings.

Sponsorship provided by

INDIANA UNIVERSITY

NSERC
CRSNG

Organizers:

Sandra Kübler, Indiana University (USA)
Gerald Penn, University of Toronto (Canada)

Program Committee:

Berthold Crysman, University of Bonn (Germany)
Amit Dubey, University of Edinburgh (UK)
Anette Frank, University of Heidelberg (Germany)
Erhard Hinrichs, University of Tübingen (Germany)
Julia Hockenmeier, University of Illinois (USA)
Laura Kallmeyer, University of Tübingen (Germany)
Frank Keller, University of Edinburgh (UK)
Wolfgang Menzel, University of Hamburg (Germany)
Stefan Müller, Free University of Berlin (Germany)
Stefan Oepen, University of Oslo (Norway)
Helmut Schmid, University of Stuttgart (Germany)
Gerold Schneider, University of Zürich (Switzerland)
Hans Uszkoreit, University of the Saarland (Germany)
Josef van Genabith, Dublin City University (Ireland)

Table of Contents

Workshop Program

Friday, June 20, 2008

8:45–9:00	Opening Remarks
9:00–9:30	*Lexicalised Parsing of German V2* Yo Sato
9:30–10:00	*Parse Selection with a German HPSG Grammar* Berthold Crysmann
10:00–10:30	*Part-of-Speech Tagging with a Symbolic Full Parser: Using the TIGER Treebank to Evaluate Fips* Yves Scherrer
10:30–11:00	Break
11:00–12:00	Invited Talk by Wolfgang Menzel
12:00–12:30	*Revisiting the Impact of Different Annotation Schemes on PCFG Parsing: A Grammatical Dependency Evaluation* Adriane Boyd and Detmar Meurers
12:30–14:00	Lunch
	Shared Task
14:00–14:30	*Parsing German with Latent Variable Grammars* Slav Petrov and Dan Klein
14:30–15:00	*Parsing Three German Treebanks: Lexicalized and Unlexicalized Baselines* Anna Rafferty and Christopher D. Manning
15:00–15:30	*A Dependency-Driven Parser for German Dependency and Constituency Representations* Johan Hall and Joakim Nivre
15:30–16:00	Break
16:00–16:30	*The PaGe 2008 Shared Task on Parsing German* Sandra Kübler

Friday, June 20, 2008 (continued)

16:30–17:30 Panel Discussion

Lexcalised Parsing of German V2

Yo Sato
Department of Computer Science
Queen Mary, University of London
Mile End Road, London E1 4NS, U.K.

Abstract

This paper presents a method and implementation of parsing German V2 word order by means of constraints that reside in lexical heads. It first describes the design of the underlying parsing engine: the head-corner chart parsing that incorporates a procedure that dynamically enforces word order constraints. While the parser could potentially generate all the permutations of terminal symbols, constraint checking is conducted *locally* in an efficient manner. The paper then shows how this parser can adequately cover a variety of V2 word order patterns with sets of lexically encoded constraints, including non-local preposing of an embedded argument or an adverbial.

1 Introduction

This paper presents a method of parsing V2 word order manifested in a variety of German matrix sentences in a lexicalised and locality-respecting manner: lexicalised, as the V2 pattern is licensed ultimately encoded in *verbs*, in the form of constraints that hold amongst its arguments and itself; locality-respecting, because (a) no constraint that operates on constituents from different subcategorisation frames is invoked and (b) the matrix verb and the preverbal constituent, however 'distant' its origin is, are ordered in the same projection via the slash-based mechanism.

The underlying grammar is loosely linearisation-based, in the sense that word order is dissociated from the syntactic structure in a discontinuity-allowing manner, as presented in Sato (2008). The main benefit of a linearisation approach is that syntactic constituency becomes independent (to a degree) of its surface realisation and hence discourages constituency manipulation for the sake of word order. In line of this spirit I will largely adopt the simple constituency construal that faithfully correspond to its semantics. However, I distance myself from the more or less standard version of linearisation grammar where potentially non-local LP conditions are permitted (Reape, 1993) or word order patterns are imposed at the clause level (as in 'topological field' model of Kathol (2000)).

The crux of the proposal consists in employing a head-corner parsing in which the set of word order constraints are incorporated into a VP's lexical head (i.e. common or auxiliary verb). For a V2 projection, its head verb contains the constraints to the effect that only one of its arguments can be fronted immediately before the verb itself. To enable this, potential discontinuity and obligatory adjacency in part of a phrase is included in the repertoire of word order constraints in addition to the standard LP (linear precedence) constraints.

2 The data

The V2 constructions to be dealt with in this paper are as follows (I will use as an example the tertiary verb gebengive or its past participle gegebengiven throughout):

1. The 'basic' case where dependency between the preverbal constituent and the matrix verb is strictly local, e.g:

Proceedings of the ACL-08: HLT Workshop on Parsing German (PaGe-08), pages 1–8,
Columbus, Ohio, USA, June 2008.

Ein Buch geben die Eltern dem Sohn.
a book give the parents the son
'A book the parents give the son'

2. The case where an argument of the lower verb is fronted across the higher auxiliary verb:

   Ein Buch haben die Eltern dem Sohn gegeben.
   a book have the parents the son given
   'A book the parents have given the son'

3. The long-distance dependency case:

   Ein Buch, sagt ein Freund, dass er glaubt, dass die Eltern dem Sohn geben.

   'A book, a friend says that he thinks that the parents give the son'

4. Adjunct fronting

   Heimlich haben die Eltern dem Sohn ein Buch gegeben.
   secretly have the parents the son a book given
   'Secretly the parents have given the son a book.'

5. Partial VP fronting

   Ein Buch dem Sohn gegeben haben die Eltern.
   Ein Buch gegeben haben die Eltern dem Sohn.

As stated, our approach adopts a linearisation approach in which constituency does not determine the surface realisation, which is handled instead by word order conditions encoded in lexical heads. My contention here is not so much plausibility as a grammar as *neutrality* to particular phrase structures, which linearisation promotes. Therefore I take a rather simplified position to use an entirely uniform phrase structure for the verb-argument structure for common verbs, namely the flat construal where all the arguments as well as the head project onto a clause ('VP') as mutual sisters, although I hasten to add our constraint enforcement could equally apply to configurational analyses. In fact we take an auxiliary verb to subcategorise for a clause rather than the complex verb analysis, and adopt the traditional binary iteration analysis for adjunct-head phrases, to see how our parser fares with configurational analyses.

I sum up the assumed constituency of the above examples graphically as trees (though this has little impact on word order):

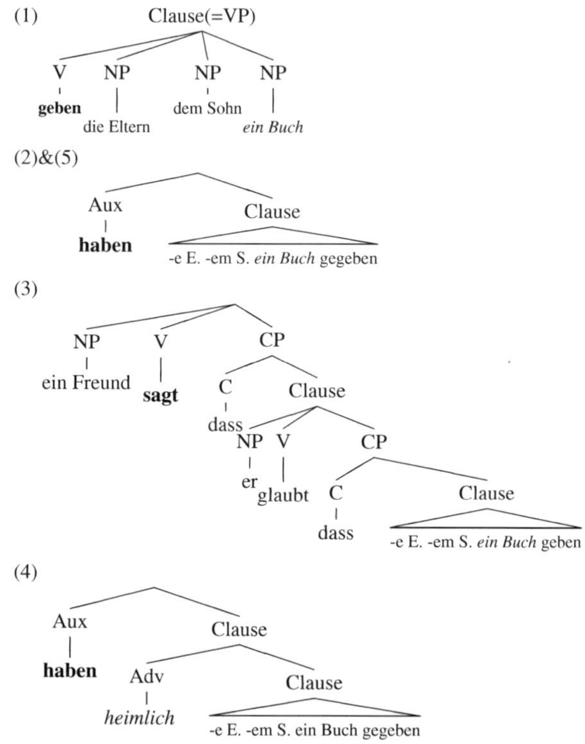

3 The parser

3.1 Core design

The design of the parser employed here can be called *constrained free word order parsing*. First, it allows for completely free word order at default. The core algorithm for the parse engine is what Reape (1991) presents as a generalised permutation-complete parser, which in turn is based on the preceding proposal of Johnson (1985). Details apart, while using context-free production rules (no multiple left-hand side non-terminal symbols), this algorithm only checks for the *presence* of all the right-hand side constituents, wherever in the string they occur, potentially discontinuously,[1] effectively licensing all the permutations of the given terminal symbols (e.g. $3! = 6$ permutations for the string consisting of *ring*, *up* and *John* including *up John ring* etc.). This 'directionless' parsing is rendered possible by Johnson's 'bitvector' representation of partial string coverage. In the above *up John ring* string, the coverage of the *ring* and *up* combina-

[1] More precisely, it searches for *non-overlapping* combinations, excluding the same word being counted more than once or more than one word counting towards the same rule in the same search path.

tion, which materially constitutes a complex verb, is represented as [1,0,1]. This is then then merged with the bitvector of *John*, [0,1,0] into [1,1,1]. Second, however, this rather promiscuous (and expensive) parsing is dynamically restricted by word order constraints that obtain in individual languages. With sufficient constraints applied during the parse, the above combinations with *ring*, *up* and *John* are restricted to *ring up John* and *ring John up*.

I do not claim for originality in this basic design. Daniels (2005) for example describes an implementation of an algorithm that falls precisely in such style of parsing.[2] The main points of the proposal lie in lexicalisation and localisation, which contrast with the general trend to introduce phrasal and non-local constraint processing for German processing, of which Daniels' work is an example. All the word order constraints are stored in lexicon, more specifically in lexical heads.

To adapt this design to a practical lexically driven parsing, the author implemented a rendering of *head-corner chart parsing*. It is head-corner in the sense described e.g. in van Noord (1991), where the parsing of a production rule always starts from its head. This is necessary for our design because the parser first retrieves the word order information from the head. Furthermore, it requires the words to be processed first by preterminal rules since without processing lexical heads the whole recognition process does not come off the ground. Therefore, a chart parsing algorithm that invokes lexical initialisation is utilised (as described in Gazdar & Mellish (1989) rather than the classical top-down parsing of Earley (1970)).

3.2 Constraint checking and propagation

Since no non-local word order constraints are introduced in our parsing, they can be fully enforced at each application of a production rule. More specifically, the checking of constraint compliance is carried out at the *completer* operation of chart parsing.[3] The data structure of an edge is suitably modified. In addition to the dotted production rule, it needs to carry the constraint set relevant to the corresponding production rule, retrievable from the head, which is always processed first in our head-corner algorithm.[4] Also, as we are adopting the bitvector representation of coverage, an edge contains its corresponding bitvector. The completer operation involves merger of two bitvectors, so the check can be conducted at this stage:

Completer in constrained parsing

Let A and B be symbols, α, β and γ be arbitrary strings, V_1 and V_2 be bitvectors and V^m be their merge, then:

If the chart contains an active edge $\langle V_1, \mathsf{A} \rightarrow \alpha \bullet \mathsf{B}\ \beta \rangle$ and a passive edge $\langle V_2, \mathsf{B} \rightarrow \gamma \bullet \rangle$, run the CHECK-ORDER procedure. If it succeeds, add edge $\langle V^m, \mathsf{A} \rightarrow \alpha\mathsf{B} \bullet \beta \rangle$ to the chart if V_1 and V_2 are mergeable. If it fails, do nothing.

The CHECK-ORDER procedure consists in a bitwise comparison of bitvectors. It picks out the bitvectors of the categories in question and checks the compliance of the newly found category with respect to the relevant constraints. If for example *A*, *B* and *C* had been found at [0,1,0,0,0], [0,0,1,0,1] and [1,0,0,1,0] respectively, this would validate $A \prec B$ but not $A \prec C$. Thus the edges for string combinations that violate the word order constraints would not be created, eliminating wasteful search paths.

As we will shortly see, the constraint type that checks continuity of a phrase is also introduced. Therefore the phrase (dis)continuity can also be ascertained *locally*, which is a major advantage over a parsing that relies largely on concatenation. Thus, the cost of constraint checking remains very small despite the capability of processing discontinuity.[5]

Note however that by locality is meant subcategorisation locality (or 'selection' locality as described in Sag (2007)): whatever is in the same subcategorisation frame of a lexical head is considered local. Depending on the adopted analysis, constituents 'local' in this sense may of course occur in different trees. Constraints on such 'non-local' —in the tree sense but not in the subcategorisation sense— constituents are still enforceable in the implemented parser. The unused constraints at a node,

[2] A foregoing implementation by Müller (2004) also employs bitvector-based linearisation approach.

[3] The equivalent operation is called the 'fundamental rule' in Gazdar & Mellish (1989).

[4] This retrieval of word order information is carried out at the *predictor* stage of chart parsing.

[5] It is worth mentioning that the bitvector checking is conducted over the whole string, the effect of applied constraints will be never lost.

for example some constraint applicable to the verb and its subject at the VP node in the configurational (subjectless-VP) analysis, is made to propagate up to the upper node. Thus it is no problem to enforce a constraint over 'different trees', as long as it is applied to 'local' constituents in our sense.[6]

4 Possible constraints and subtyping

It is crucial, if the computational properties of the parser is to be transparent in constrained free word order parsing, to identify the kind of word order constraints admitted into lexical heads. We will remain relatively conservative, in introducing only two operators for constraint encoding. We first invoke the binary LP operator ($\prec$) in a conventional sense: the whole (or, equivalently, right-periphery) of a string for category *A* needs to precede the whole (or left-periphery) of a string for category *B* to satisfy $A \prec B$ (I will use the shorthand $A \prec (B, C)$ to express $(A \prec B) \wedge (A \prec C)$. Crucially, the contiguity operator () is added. It takes a *set* of constituents as its operand and requires the constituents in it to be contiguous, regardless of their order. Thus, $\{A, B, C\}$ encodes the requirement for A, B and C *as a whole* forming a contiguous string. For example, the string *I ring John up* does not satisfy $\{ring, up\}$ but does satisfy $\{ring, John, up\}$.

Also important is how to succinctly generalise on the word order patterns now encoded in lexical items, as one would certainly want to avoid a tedious task of writing them all individually, if they allow for broader classification. For example the English transitive verb generally follows its subject argument and precedes its object argument, and one would naturally want to lump these verbs under one umbrella. For such a cluster of lexical heads, we will introduce a *word order (sub)type*. More pertinently, the German verbs may be classified into *v1-verb*, *v2-verb* and *vf-verb* according to the positions of their arguments in their projection. We will also allow *multiple inheritance* that becomes standard in the typed feature system (cf. Pollard and Sag (1987)).

[6]See Sato (2006) for details.

5 Constraints for V2

5.1 General setup

To enforce the V2 word order pattern lexically, I propose to use a combination of two word order subtypes: *dislocating-verb* (*disl-v*) and *matrix-v2-verb* (*mtrx-v2-v*). The former type represents a verb one of whose arguments is to be 'dislocated'. A verb of this type can thus be characterised as 'contributing' the dislocated (preverbal) element. The latter, on the other hand, is the type that is projected onto a matrix sentence. This type should be constrained such that one dislocated constituent must —and only one may— precede and be adjacent to the verb itself. It may be characterised as a verb that provides a locus —immediately before itself— of, or 'receives' the dislocated element.

Dislocation is handled by a constraint percolation mechanism. I assume the dislocated constituent is pushed into a storage that then participates in a slash style percolation, although the storage content would still need to be ordered by lexicalised constraints rather than by the percolation mechanism itself, as they are the sole resource for word order.[7] Thus the checking as regards the dislocated constituent is conducted at each projection in the percolation path, hence locally, while the percolation mechanism gives some 'global' control over dislocation. Not just the positioning of the dislocated constituent at the left-periphery of the whole sentence, but the assurance of a *global* singularity restriction of dislocation —not just one constituent per clause in multiple embeddings— becomes thus possible.

Let args be the set of the arguments of a *disl-v*, disl be that of the dislocated one and situ be that of the remaining arguments, i.e. $\mathsf{disl} \subset \mathsf{args}$ where $|\mathsf{disl}| = 1$ and $\mathsf{situ} = \{x | x \in \mathsf{args} \wedge x \notin \mathsf{disl}\}$. Then the type *disl-v* can be characterised as having the following constraint:

disl-v: $\mathsf{disl} \prec \mathsf{situ} \quad (\mathsf{disl} \rightarrow \mathsf{disl}_{st})$

Simply put, this says that the arguments are divided into two parts, the dislocated and in-situ parts, the former of which precedes the latter. We assume, as

[7]The adopted mechanism is close to Penn (1999), though he invokes potentially non-local topology-based constraints and removes the filler and gapped head entirely.

in the standard treatment, there is only one dislocated constituent, until we consider the VP fronting. The notation with an arrow on the right indicates this singleton set is pushed into the storage that is propagated upwards.

The *mtrx-v2-v* type is then characterised as follows:

mtrx-v2-v: $\mathsf{disl}_{st} \prec \mathsf{verb}, \ \{\mathsf{disl}_{st}, \mathsf{verb}\}$

This simply says the dislocated constituent (stored in a lower node and percolated) immediately precedes the matrix verb. (For the following presentation, the storage-related notations will be omitted and implicitly assumed unless necessary. Also, the set variables disl and args will be used with the same meaning.)

Thus the combination of the two types gives, for example where $\mathsf{args} = \{A, B, C\}$, $\mathsf{disl} = \{A\}$ and the matrix verb is V, the following constraint set:

$$\{A \prec (B, C), \ \ A \prec V, \ \{A, V\}\}$$

which essentially says that the dislocated A immediately precedes the matrix verb V and precedes (not necessarily immediately) the in-situ B and C.

5.2 Local case

To begin with, let us see a case where dependency between the preverbal constituent and the matrix verb is strictly local, taking (1) as an example. Note first that there are six possible variants:

(1)

a. Die Eltern geben dem Sohn ein Buch.
b. Die Eltern geben ein Buch dem Sohn.
c. Dem Sohn geben die Eltern ein Buch.
d. Dem Sohn geben ein Buch die Eltern.
e. Ein Buch geben die Eltern dem Sohn.
f. Ein Buch geben dem Sohn die Eltern.

In this case, *geben* is both a matrix (argument-receiving) and dislocating (argument-contributing) verb. This means that the two subtypes should be overloaded. Let us call this overloaded sub-species *disl-mtrx-v2-v*: which is given the following specification:

disl-mtrx-v2-v:
$\mathsf{disl} \prec \mathsf{situ}, \ \ \mathsf{disl} \prec \mathsf{verb}, \ \ \{\mathsf{disl}, \mathsf{verb}\}$

To adapt this type to our verb, *geben*, where we represent its arguments as sNP (subject NP), ioNP (indirect object NP) and doNP (direct object NP), we obtain, for the case where sNP is preposed:

$\{\mathsf{sNP} \prec (\mathsf{ioNP}, \mathsf{doNP}),$
$\ \mathsf{sNP} \prec \mathsf{geben}, \ \ (\mathsf{sNP}, \mathsf{geben})\}$

where the constraints on the first line is inherited from *disloc-v* while those on the second from *matrix-v2-v*. This corresponds to the sentences (a) and (b) above. The followings are the cases where ioNP and doNP are preposed, corresponding to (c,d) and (e,f), respectively.

$\{\mathsf{ioNP} \prec (\mathsf{sNP}, \mathsf{doNP}), \ \ \mathsf{ioNP} \prec \mathsf{geben}, \ \ (\mathsf{ioNP}, \mathsf{geben})\}$
$\{\mathsf{doNP} \prec (\mathsf{sNP}, \mathsf{ioNP}), \ \ \mathsf{doNP} \prec \mathsf{geben}, \ \ (\mathsf{doNP}, \mathsf{geben})\}$

These possible sets are enforced in the manner of exclusive disjunction, that is, only one of the above three sets actually obtains. This does not mean, however, each set must be explicitly stated in the verb and processed blindly. Only the abstract form of the constraint, as described under the type specification above, is written in the lexicon. During parsing, then, one of the sets, as dynamically found to match the input string, is computed and applied. In the subsequent discussion, therefore, only the direct-object fronting case is considered as a representative example for each construction.

5.3 Argument fronting across auxiliary

We now consider the cases where the dependency is not local, starting with an auxiliary-involving case. The dependency between an auxiliary and an argument of its lower verb is, according to the Aux-Clause construal adopted here, is not local. We can however succinctly specify such non-local V2 renderings as a case where the above two types are instantiated separately in two verbs. The example is reproduced below:

(2) Ein Buch haben die Eltern dem Sohn gegeben.

The argument-contributing gegebengiven is, as before, assigned the *disl-v* type, but is further subtyped and inherits the constraints also from *vf-v* (v-final verb), reflecting the fact that it occurs head-finally.

gegeben (type *disl-vf-v*):
$\{\mathsf{doNP} \prec (\mathsf{sNP}, \mathsf{ioNP}),$

$(\mathsf{sNP}, \mathsf{doNP}, \mathsf{ioNP}) \prec \mathsf{gegeben}\}$

The dislocated doNP climbs up the tree ((2) in Section 2) in the storage, which is then subject to the constraints of matrix *haben* at the top node. This argument-receiving auxiliary *haben* is, as before, given the *mtrx-v2-v* status.[8].

haben (type *mtrx-v2-v*):
$\{\mathsf{doNP}_{st} \prec \mathsf{haben}, (\mathsf{doNP}_{st}, \mathsf{haben})\}$

Thus the dislocated *ein Buch* is duly placed at the left-periphery in a manner that forbids intervention between itself and the matrix verb.

5.4 Long-Distance Dependency

Having dealt with an argument fronting of the auxiliary construction as a non-local case, we could now extend the same treatment to long-distance dependency. Our example is:

(3) Ein Buch, sagt ein Freund, dass er glaubt, dass die Eltern dem Sohn geben.

('A book, a friend says that he thinks that the parents give the son')

In fact, it suffices to endow exactly the same type as *gegeben*, i.e. *disl-vf-v*, to the occurrence of *geben* in a subordinate clause.[9]

geben (in subord. clause, type *disl-vf-v*):
$\{\mathsf{doNP} \prec (\mathsf{sNP}, \mathsf{ioNP}),$
$(\mathsf{sNP}, \mathsf{doNP}, \mathsf{ioNP}) \prec \mathsf{geben}\}$

This ensures that the dislocated argument goes progressively up towards the top node. To prevent this argument from being 'dropped' the half way through, however, the non-matrix CP-taking verbs 'in the middle' that should be bypassed, in our case *glaubt*, needs to possess the constraint that pushes the dislocated element to the left of itself:

glaubt (in subord. clause, type '*middle-v*'):[10]
$\{\mathsf{doNP}_{st} \prec \mathsf{glaubt}\}$

Finally, a *mtrx-v2-v*, in our case *sagt*, takes care of placing the dislocated constituent immediately before itself.

sagt (type *mtrx-v2-v*):[11]
$\{\mathsf{doNP}_{st} \prec \mathsf{sagt}, (\mathsf{doNP}_{st}, \mathsf{sagt})\}$

5.5 Adjunct fronting

I declared at the beginning to use the traditional binary adjunction analysis for adjunct-head phrases.[12] In order to achieve this, I first propose a fundamental conceptual shift, given the iterability and optionality of adjuncts. In the traditional concept of adjunct-head phrases, it is the adjunct that selects for the head it modifies rather than the other way round. Also semantically, the adjunct is considered the 'semantic head' that works as a functor. In light of this background, it is not implausible to take the adjunct as the 'parsing head' equipped with word order constraints. In fact, the opposite option — equipping the syntactic head with its relative word order with adjuncts— is not as feasible in our lexical head-corner parsing. The iterability of adjuncts means that the head would have to be equipped with an infinite number of adjuncts as its 'arguments', which would lead to various uninstantiation problems. Therefore, I swap the statuses and treat, in terms of parsing, the adjunct as a functor with word order constraints incorporated relative to its modifiee.

Thus, the word order constraints are now given to the lexical adjuncts also. I will take as an example adverbs.[13] Adverbs are now the potential locus of word order patterns relative to its modifiee (clause/VP), but are not given any specific constraint in German generally, because one can appear either after or inside a clause. Our focus is solely on the possibility of putting one *before* the clause it modifies, when it is subject to the V2 constraint. This is handled simply by saying, for such a type, which we call *disl-adverb*, it *dislocates itself*, in the manner of

[8]More precisely this also involves $\mathsf{haben} \prec \mathsf{VP}$(gapped)

[9]This means that, given the identical morphological form, *gegeben* is type-ambiguous between the matrix and subordinate occurrences. This does not add too much to parsing complexity, however, as this 'ambiguity' is quickly resolved when one of its argument is encountered.

[10]The constraints applicable to the usual finite verb is omitted, i.e. $\mathsf{sNP} \prec \mathsf{glaubt}$ and $\mathsf{glaubt} \prec \mathsf{CP}$(gapped).

[11]Likewise: $\mathsf{sagt} \prec \mathsf{CP}$(gapped) omitted.

[12]That is against the temptation for a constituency change that renders adjuncts sisters on par with arguments (cf. Bouma et al (2001)), in which case V2 would simply fall out from the foregoing word order types.

[13]The same treatment can be extended to prepositional adjuncts (remember the unused constraints will percolate up to the maximal projection).

'head movement' which is widely used in German syntax (Kiss and Wesche, 1991; Netter, 1992).

disl-adverb: adv (adv$\rightarrow$ disl$_{st}$)

This specification ensures the adverb itself goes onto the extraction path, to be placed at the left-periphery, triggered by the *mtrx-v2-v* type. The singularity of the adverbials at the prerverbal position is ensured by means of percolation storage control.

6 Verbal Fronting

Our last challenge concerns fronting of verb or verbal projections. From the preceding discussion, an option that suggests itself is to treat the verb fronting as the case of verb dislocating itself. I will indeed propose a strategy along this line, but this avenue proves more difficult due to complications specific to verb-related fronting. Firstly, generally such fronting is limited to the environment of a lower VP governed by a higher verb such as an auxiliary, as can be seen from the following contrast:

(4)

a. Gegeben haben die Eltern dem Sohn ein Buch.

b. *Geben, sagt ein Freund, dass die Eltern dem Sohn ein Buch.

Second, the type we used for *gegeben* in Section 5.3, namely *disl-vf-v*, clearly does not work, as the verb does not occur phrase-finally (but in fact initially) relative to its sisters in (4a). Some relaxation of LP constraints seem to be in order.

Thirdly, German displays a variety of ways to front *part* of a VP:

(5)

Gegeben haben die Eltern dem Sohn ein Buch.
Dem Sohn gegeben haben die Eltern ein Buch.
Ein Buch gegeben haben die Eltern dem Sohn.
Dem Sohn ein Buch gegeben haben die Eltern.

This raises the question of whether this fits in the V2 pattern at all, coupled with the ongoing debate on the status of the preverbal string. Quite apart from the theoretical debate, however, how best to adequately generate these patterns is an acute parsing issue. We are assuming the flat clause=VP anaylsis, so relaxing the singularity condition seems unavoidable.

Fourthly, to make the matter worse, allowing multiple frontings and dropping LP requirements does not solve the problem, as ordering of the preverbal constituents is constrained, as shown in the following data:

(6)

*Gegeben dem Sohn haben die Eltern ein Buch.
*Dem Sohn gegeben ein Buch haben die Eltern.

It is a great challenge for any syntactician to provide a unified account for such complex behaviour, and I confine myself here to offering the 'solution' sets of constraints that adequately generate the desired string. What I offer is this: allowing multiple dislocations only for the verbal fronting cases via a new word order subtype, while retaining the verb-final LP conditions for these dislocated constituents.

For this new type we first relax the singularity condition for dislocation. To allow multiple dislocations, it would suffice to drop the $|\mathsf{disl}| = 1$ condition, but an unrestricted application of disl $\subset$ args would lead to overgeneration, due to two further constraints applicable: (1) not *all* arguments can and (2) the subject argument cannot be fronted along with the verb (as in (a) and (b) below, respectively):

(7)

a. *Die Eltern dem Sohn ein Buch gegeben haben.

b. *Die Eltern gegeben haben dem Sohn ein Buch.
*Die Eltern ein Buch gegeben haben dem Sohn.

Therefore we add the conditions to exlude the above, along with the the verb-final constraint applicable the dislocated constituents to exclude (6). Let us call this type *frontable-v*. The constraint specification is as follows:

gegeben (*frontable-v*):
$\mathsf{disl} = \{\mathsf{gegeben}\} \cup \mathsf{ptargs},\ \ \mathsf{ptargs} \prec \mathsf{gegeben}$
where ptargs $\subset$ args and sNP $\notin$ ptargs

The proposed constraint set might strike as rather *ad hoc*. It would clearly be better to treat both the fronted and non-fronted occurrences of *gegeben* as sharing some common word order type, and what is meant by 'applying the constraints amongst the dislocated constituents' needs to be fleshed out. Thus this may not be an elegant solution, but nevertheless is an generatively adequate solution. More importantly it serves as a good example for the flexibility and adaptability of constrained free word order parsing, because it handles a rather complex word order pattern in a way neutral to grammatical construal, i.e. without invoking constituency manipulation.

7 Concluding Remarks

I conclude this paper by responding to a natural objection: why would one have to go through this convoluted route of lexical word order control, when the 'natural' way to constrain V2 —or V1 and VF, for that matter— would be to have some 'global' patterns pertinent to clause types? My responses are primarily engineering-oriented. First, lexicalised encoding gives the parser, through locality restriction, a certain control over computational complexity, as the search space for constraint enforcement is restricted.[14] However this not an entirely unique, if more amenable, feature to lexicalised parsing, as one could impose such a control in non-lexicalised parsing. The advantage truly unique to lexicalising word order lies in rendering the parser and grammar independent of surface realisation and hence re-usable across languages. In short, it promotes modularity. As we have seen, though the parser needs to conform to a certain strategy, the word order component is fairly independent, as a separate procedure which can be modified if for example more types of word order operators are needed. The grammar could also be kept more compact and cross-linguistically applicable, because word order is abstracted away from constituency. Therefore, paradoxically, an advantage of lexicalising German parsing is to enable the same parser/grammar to be used in other languages too, even if it is not naturally suited to the language.

References

Gosse Bouma, Robert Malouf, and Ivan Sag. 2001. Satisfying constraints on extraction and adjunction. *Natural Language and Linguistic Theory*, 19(1).

Mike Daniels. 2005. *Generalized ID/LP Grammar*. Ph.D. thesis, Ohio State University.

Jay Earley. 1970. An efficient context free parsing algorithm. *Communications of ACM*, 13:94–102.

Gerald Gazdar and Chris Mellish. 1989. *Natural Language Processing in Prolog*. Addison Wesley.

Mark Johnson. 1985. Parsing with discontinuous constituents. In *Proceedings of the 23rd Annual Meeting of the ACL*, pages 127–132.

Andreas Kathol. 2000. *Linear Syntax*. OUP.

Tibor Kiss and B Wesche. 1991. Verb order and head movement. In O Herzog, editor, *Text Understanding in LILOG*, pages 216–40. Springer.

Stefan Müller. 2004. Continuous or discontinuous constituents? a comparison between syntactic analyses for constituent order and their processing systems. *Research on Language and Computation 2(2)*.

Klaus Netter. 1992. On non-head non-movement. An HPSG treatment of finite verb position in German. In G. Görz, editor, *Proceedings of KONVENS 92*. Springer.

Gerald Penn. 1999. Linearization and Wh-extraction in HPSG: Evidence from Serbo-Croatian. In R. Borsely and A. Przepiorkowski, editors, *Slavic in HPSG*. CSLI.

Carl Pollard and Ivan Sag. 1987. *Information-Based Syntax and Semantics*. CSLI.

Mike Reape. 1991. Parsing bounded discontinuous constituents: Generalisation of some common algorithms. *DIANA Report, Edinburgh University*.

Mike Reape. 1993. *A Formal Theory of Word Order*. Ph.D. thesis, Edinburgh University.

Ivan Sag. 2007. Remarks on locality. In Stefan Müller, editor, *Proceedings of HPSG07*. CSLI.

Yo Sato. 2006. A proposed lexicalised linearisation grammar: a monostratal alternative. In Stefan Müller, editor, *Proceedings of HPSG06*. CSLI.

Yo Sato. 2008. *Implementing Head-Driven Linearisation Grammar*. Ph.D. thesis, King's College London.

Oliver Suhre. 1999. Computational Aspects of a Grammar Formalism for Languages with Freer Word Order. Diplomarbeit, Eberhard-Karls-Universität Tübingen.

Gertjan van Noord. 1991. Head corner parsing for discontinuous constituency. In *Proceedings of the 29th annual meeting on ACL*, pages 114–121.

[14] For a complexity analysis of such grammar, see Sato (2008) and Suhre (1999).

Parse selection with a German HPSG grammar

Berthold Crysmann*

Institut für Kommunikationswissenschaften, Universität Bonn &
Computerlinguistik, Universität des Saarlandes
Poppelsdorfer Allee 47
D-55113 Bonn

crysmann@ifk.uni-bonn.de

Abstract

We report on some recent parse selection experiments carried out with GG, a large-scale HPSG grammar for German. Using a manually disambiguated treebank derived from the Verbmobil corpus, we achieve over 81% exact match accuracy compared to a 21.4% random baseline, corresponding to an error reduction rate of 3.8.

1 Introduction

The literature on HPSG parsing of German has almost exclusively been concerned with issues of theoretical adequacy and parsing efficiency. In contrast to LFG parsing of German, or even to HPSG work on English or Japanese, very little effort has been spent on the question of how the intended, or, for that matter a likely parse, can be extracted from the HPSG parse forest of some German sentence. This issue becomes all the more pressing, as the grammars gain in coverage, inevitably increasing their ambiguity. In this paper, I shall present preliminary results on probabilistic parse selection for a large-scale HPSG of German, building on technology developed in the Lingo Redwoods project (Oepen et al., 2002).

The paper is organised as follows: in section 2, I shall give a brief overview of the grammar. Section 3 discusses the treebanking effort we have undertaken (3.1), followed by a presentation of the parse selection results we achieve using probabilistic models trained on different feature sets (3.2).

2 The grammar

The grammar used in the experiments reported here has originally been developed, at DFKI, in the context of the Verbmobil project (Müller and Kasper, 2000). Developed initially for the PAGE development and processing platform (Uszkoreit et al., 1994), the grammar has subsequently been ported to LKB (Copestake, 2001) and Pet (Callmeier, 2000) by Stefan Müller. Since 2002, the grammar has been extended and modified by Berthold Crysmann (Crysmann, 2003; Crysmann, 2005; Crysmann, 2007).

The grammar, codename GG, is a large scale HPSG grammar for German, freely available under an open-source license: it consists of roughly 4000 types, out of which 290 are parametrised lexical types, used in the definition of about 35,000 lexical entries. The lexicon is further extended by 44 lexical rules and about 300 inflectional rules. On the syntactic side, the grammar has about 80 phrase structure rules.

The grammar covers all major aspects of German clausal and phrasal syntax, including free word order in the clausal domain, long-distance dependencies, complex predicates, passives, and extraposition (Crysmann, 2005). Furthermore, the grammar covers different coordination constructions, including

*The research reported here has been carried out at the German Research Center for Artificial Intelligence (DFKI GmbH) as part of the projects COLLATE, QALL-ME, and Checkpoint, funded by the German Federal Ministery for education and Science (BMBF), the European Union, and the State of Berlin, respectively. I am also greatly indepted to my colleagues Bernd Kiefer and Günter Neumann, as well as to Stephan Oepen and Dan Flickinger for support and comments relating to the work presented here.

Proceedings of the ACL-08: HLT Workshop on Parsing German (PaGe-08), pages 9–15,
Columbus, Ohio, USA, June 2008. ©2008 Association for Computational Linguistics

the so-called SGF coordination. Furthermore, the grammar is fully reversible, i.e. it can be used for parsing, as well as generation.

The phrase structure rules of the grammar are either unary or binary branching phrase structure schemata, permitting free interspersal of modifiers between complements in the clausal domain. The relatively free order of complements is captured by means of lexical rules which permute the elements on the COMPS valence list. As a result, the verb's complements can be saturated in any order.

The treatment of verb placement is somewhat special: in sentences without a right sentence bracket, a left branching structure is assumed, permitting efficient processing. Whenever the right bracket is occupied by a non-finite verb cluster, the finite verb in the left bracket is related to the clause finla cluster by means of simulated head movement, following the proposal by (Kiss and Wesche, 1991), inter alia. As a consequence, the grammar provides both head-initial and head-final versions of the Head-Adjunct, Head-Complement and Head-Subject schemata.

As output, the grammar delivers detailed semantic representations in the form of Minimal Recursion Semantics (Copestake et al., 2005). These representations have been successfully used in the context of automated email response or question answering (Frank et al., 2006). Most recently, the grammar has been used for automatic correction of grammar and style errors, combining robust parsing with generation.

3 Parse Selection

3.1 Treebank construction

The treebank used in the experiments reported here has been derived from the German subset of the Verbmobil (Wahlster, 2000) corpus. In essence, we removed any duplicates on the string level from the corpus, in order to reduce the amount of subsequent manual annotation. Many of the duplicates thus removed were short interjection, such as *ja* "yes", *nein* "no", or *hm* "euhm", which do not give rise to any interesting structural ambiguities. As a side effect, removal of these duplicates also enhanced the quality of the resulting treebank.

The construction of the disambiguated treebank for German followed the procedure suggested for English by (Oepen et al., 2002): the corpus was first analysed with the German HPSG GG, storing the derivation trees of all successful parses. In a subsequent annotation step, we manually selected the best parse, if any, from the parse forest, using the Redwoods annotation tool cited above.

After removal of duplicates, syntactic coverage of the corpus figured at 69.3 percent, giving a total of 11894 out of 16905 sentences. The vast majority of sentences in the corpus are between 1 and 15 words in length (14757): as a result, average sentence length of parsed utterances figures at 7.64, compared to 8.72 for the entire corpus. Although average sentence length is comparatively low, the treebank still contains items up to sentence length 47.

The 11894 successfully parsed sentences have subsequently been disambiguated with the Redwoods treebanking tool, which is built on top of LKB (Copestake, 2001) and [incr tsdb()] (Oepen, 2002). Figure 2 shows the annotation of an example sentence from the treebank.

During annotation, 10356 sentences were successfully disambiguated to a single reading (87.1%). Another 276 sentences were also disambiguated, yet contain some unresolved ambiguity (2.3%), while 95 sentences were left unannotated (0.8%). The remaining 1167 items (=9.8%) were rejected, since the parse forest did not contain the desired reading. Since not all test items in the tree bank were ambiguous, we were left, after manual disambiguation, with 8230 suitable test items, i.e. test items where the number of readings assigned by the parser exceeds the number of readings judged as acceptable.

Average ambiguity of fully disambiguated sentences in the tree bank is around 12.7 trees per sentence. This corresponds to a baseline of 21.4% for random parse selection, owing to the unequal distribution of low and high ambiguity sentences.

3.2 Parse selection

3.2.1 Feature selection

The parse selection experiments reported on here have been performed using the LOGON branch of the LKB and [incr tsdb()] systems. In particular, we used Rob Malouf's tadm maximum entropy toolkit for training and evaluation of our log-linear parse selection models.

Aggregate	all results			t–active = 0			t–active = 1			t–active > 1			unannotated		
	items #	words Ø	trees Ø	items #	words Ø	trees Ø	items #	words Ø	trees Ø	items #	words Ø	trees Ø	items #	words Ø	trees Ø
i–length in [45 .. 50|	2	47.00	800.0	0	0.00	0.0	2	46.00	800.0	0	0.00	0.0	0	0.00	0.0
i–length in [35 .. 40|	6	36.78	545.2	5	37.60	327.0	1	36.00	1636.0	0	0.00	0.0	0	0.00	0.0
i–length in [30 .. 35|	20	31.63	211.1	11	32.00	226.3	8	30.50	212.5	0	0.00	0.0	1	30.00	33.0
i–length in [25 .. 30|	56	26.70	377.5	26	26.58	508.3	27	26.41	282.7	3	25.67	98.0	0	0.00	0.0
i–length in [20 .. 25|	172	21.54	173.0	69	21.72	203.4	99	21.52	136.2	2	20.50	92.0	2	20.00	1023.5
i–length in [15 .. 20|	650	16.58	70.1	185	16.59	81.3	447	16.35	65.4	11	17.27	63.5	7	16.71	76.6
i–length in [10 .. 15|	2100	11.63	24.8	333	11.83	40.2	1706	11.43	21.3	24	11.33	28.5	37	11.51	44.2
i–length in [5 .. 10|	6227	6.84	6.3	455	7.24	10.2	5641	6.74	5.9	89	7.00	10.1	42	7.05	9.3
i–length in [0 .. 5|	2661	3.16	2.8	83	3.63	3.8	2418	3.21	2.6	154	1.44	5.8	6	3.67	1.7
Total	11894	9.07	17.2	1167	11.43	55.5	10349	7.32	12.7	283	5.04	12.9	95	9.80	49.0

(generated by [incr tsdb()] at 24–mar–08 (22:28))

Figure 1: The GG Verbmobil treebank

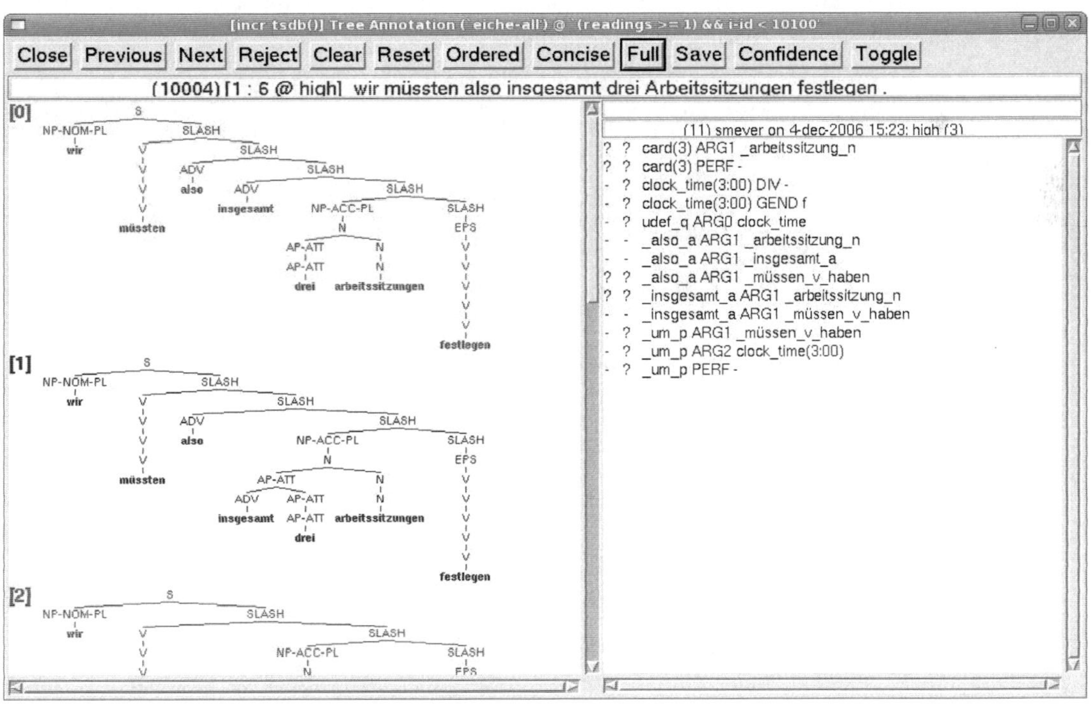

Figure 2: An example from the German treebank, featuring the Redwoods annotation tool

All experiments were carried out as a ten-fold cross-evaluation with 10 iterations, using 10 different sets of 7407 annotated sentences for training and 10 disjoint sets of 823 test items for testing.

The discriminative models we evaluate here were trained on different subsets of features, all of which were extracted from the rule backbone of the derivations stored in the treebank. As node labels, we used the names of the HPSG rules licensing a phrasal node, as well as the types of lexical entries (preterminals). On the basis of these derivation trees, we selected several features for training our disambiguation models: local trees of depth 1, several levels of grandparenting, i.e. inclusion of grandparent node (GP 2), great-grandparent node (GP 3) and great-great-grandparent node (GP 4), partial trees of depth 1 (+AE). Grandparenting features involve local trees of depth 1 plus a sequence of grandparent nodes, i.e. the local tree is contextualised in relation to the dominating tree. Information about a grandparent's other daughters, however, is not taken into consideration. Partial trees, by contrast, are included as a kind of back-off model.

In addition to tree-configurational features, we experimented with n-gram models, using n-gram sizes between 2 and 4. These models were further varied, according to whether or not a back-off model was included.

Apart from these linguistic features, we also varied two parameters of the maximum entropy learner, viz. variance and relative tolerance. The relative tolerance parameter restricts convergence of the model, whereas variance defines a prior in order to reduce over-fitting. In the results reported here, we used optimal setting for each individual set of linguistic parameters, although, in most cases, these optimal values figured at 10^{-4} for variance and 10^{-6} for relative tolerance.

3.2.2 Results

The results of our parse selection experiments for German are summarised in tables 1 and 2, as well as figures 3 and 4.

As our major result, we can report an exact match accuracy for parse selection of 81.72%, using great-grandparenting (GP 3) and 4-grams. This result corresponds to an error reduction by a factor of 3.8, as compared to the 21.4% random baseline.

	−AE	+AE
GP 0	77.96	78.14
GP 2	81.27	80.87
GP 3	81.34	80.4
GP 4	81.49	80.78

Table 1: PCFG model with Grandparenting

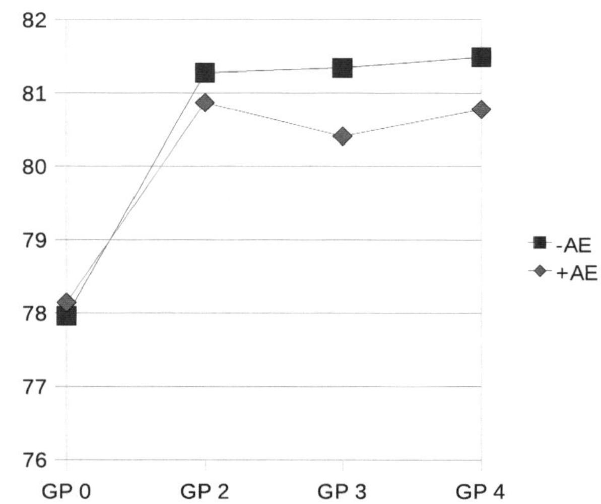

Figure 3: PCFG model with Grandparenting

Apart from the overall result in terms of achievable parse selection accuracy, a comparison of the individual results is also highly informative.

As illustrated by figure 3, models including any level of grandparenting clearly outperform the basic model without grandparenting (GP0). Furthermore, relative gains with increasing levels of grandparenting are quite low, compared to the more than 3% increase in accuracy between the GP0 and GP2 models.

Another interesting observation regarding the data in table 1 and figure 3 is that the inclusion of partial constituents into the model (+AE) only benefits the most basic model. Once the more sophisticated grandparenting models are used, partial constituent worsen rather than improve the overall performance.

Another observation we made regarding the relative usefulness of the features we have employed relates to n-gram models: again, we find that n-gram models clearly improve on the basic model without grandparenting (by about 1 percentage point), albeit to a lesser degree than grandparenting itself (see

	N0	N2	N3	N4
GP 0	77.96	78.79	78.92	78.74
GP 2	81.27	81.5	81.65	81.55
GP 3	81.34	81.44	81.51	81.72
GP 4	81.49	81.62	81.69	81.67

Table 2: PCFG model with Grandparenting & N-grams

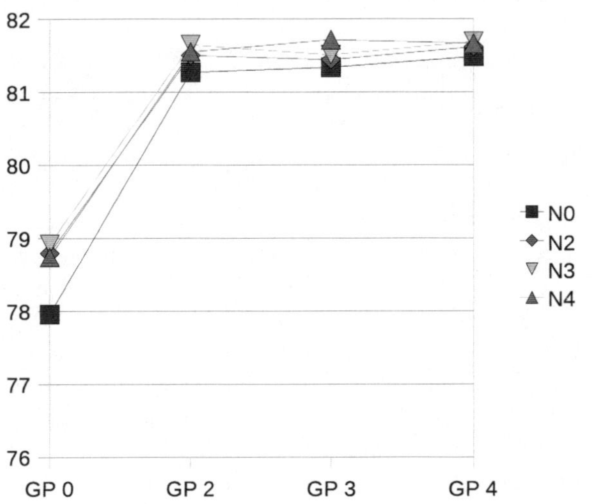

Figure 4: PCFG model with Grandparenting & N-Grams (-AE)

above). With grandparenting added, however, the relative gains of the n-gram models greatly diminishes. A possible explanation for this finding is that reference to grandparenting indirectly makes available information about the preceding and linear context, obviating the need for direct encoding in terms of n-grams. Again, the best combined model (hierarchy + n-grams) outperforms the best purely hierarchical model by a mere 0.23 percentage points. The results obtained here for German thus replicate the results established earlier for English, namely that the inclusion of n-gram information only improves overall parse selection to a less significant extent.

A probably slightly unsurprising result relates to the use of back-off models: we found that n-gram models with backing-off yielded better results throughout our test field than the correspoding n-gram models that did not use this feature. Differences, however, were not dramatic, ranging roughly between 0.07 and 0.3 percentage points.

The results obtained here for German compare quite well to the results previously achieved for the ERG, a broad coverage HPSG for English: using a similar treebank[1] (Toutanova et al., 2002) report 81.80 exact match accuracy for a log-linear model with local trees plus ancestor information, the model which is closest to the models we have evaluated here. The baseline in their experiments is 25.81. The best model they obtain includes semantic dependencies, as well, yielding 82.65 exact match accuracy.

Probably the most advanced approach to parse selection for German is (Forst, 2007): using a broad coverage LFG grammar, he reports an f-score of 83% of correctly assigned dependency triples for a reference corpus of manually annotated newspaper text. However, it is unclear how these figures relate to the exact match accuracy used here.

Relevant, in principle, to our discussion here, are also the results obtained with treebank grammars for German: (Dubey and Keller, 2003) have trained a PCFG on the Negra corpus (Skut et al., 1998), reporting labelled precision and recall between 70 and 75%. (Kübler et al., 2006) essentially confirm these results for the Negra treebank, but argue instead that probabilistic parsing for German can reach far better results (around 89%), once a different treebank is chosen, e.g. Tüba-D/Z. However, it is quite difficult to interpret the significance of these two treebank parsers for our purposes here: not only is the evaluation metric an entirely different one, but so are the parsing task and the corpus.

In an less recent paper, however, (Ruland, 2000) reports on probabilistic parsing of Verbmobil data using a probabilistic LR-parser. The parser has been trained on a set of 19,750 manually annotated sentences. Evaluation of the parser was then performed on a hold-out set of 1000 sentences. In addition to labelled precision and recall, (Ruland, 2000) also report exact match, which figures at 46.3%. Using symbolic postprocessing, exact match improves to as much as 53.8%. Table 3.2.2 summarizes Ruland's results, permitting a comparison between exact match and PARSEVAL measures. Although the test sets are certainly not fully comparable,[2] these

[1] In fact, the Redwoods treebank used by (Toutanova et al., 2002) was also derived from Verbmobil data. The size of the treebank, however, is somewhat smaller, containing a total of 5312 sentences.

[2] The overall size of the treebank suggests that we are ac-

	German
Not parsed	4.3%
Exact match	53.8%
LP	90.8%
LR (all)	84.9%
LR (in coverage)	91.6%

Table 3: Performance of Ruland's probabilistic parser (with postprocessing) on Verbmobil data

figures at least gives us an indication about how to judge the the performance of the HPSG parse selection models presented here: multiplying our 69.3% coverage with 81.72% exact match accuracy still gives us an overall exact match accuracy of 56.6% for the entire corpus.

However, comparing our German treebank to a structurally similar English treebank, we have shown that highly comparable parse selection figures can be obtained for the two languages with essentially the same type of probabilistic model.

4 Conclusion

We have presented a treebanking effort for a large-scale German HPSG grammar, built with the Redwoods treebank technology (Oepen et al., 2002), and discussed some preliminary parse selection results that are comparable in performance to the results previously achieved for the English Resource Grammar (lingoredwoods:2002tlt). Using a treebank of 8230 disambiguated sentences, we trained discriminative log-linear models that achieved a maximal exact match accuracy of 81.69%, against a random baseline of 21.4%. We further investigated the impact of different levels of grandparenting and n-grams, and found that inclusion of the grandparent node into the model improved the quality significantly, reference, however, to any higher nodes only lead to very mild improvements. For n-grams we could only observe significant gains for models without any grandparenting. We therefore hope to test these findings against treebanks with a higher syntactic complexity, in the near future, in order to establish whether these observations are indeed robust.

tually dealing with the same set of primary data. However, in our HPSG treebank string-identical test items had been removed prior to annotation and training. As a result, our treebank contains less redundancy than the original Verbmobil test suites.

References

Ulrich Callmeier. 2000. PET — a platform for experimentation with efficient HPSG processing techniques. *Journal of Natural Language Engineering*, 6(1):99–108.

Ann Copestake, Dan Flickinger, Carl Pollard, and Ivan Sag. 2005. Minimal recursion semantics: an introduction. *Research on Language and Computation*, 3(4):281–332.

Ann Copestake. 2001. *Implementing Typed Feature Structure Grammars*. CSLI Publications, Stanford.

Berthold Crysmann. 2003. On the efficient implementation of German verb placement in HPSG. In *Proceedings of RANLP 2003*, pages 112–116, Borovets, Bulgaria.

Berthold Crysmann. 2005. Relative clause extraposition in German: An efficient and portable implementation. *Research on Language and Computation*, 3(1):61–82.

Berthold Crysmann. 2007. Local ambiguity packing and discontinuity in german. In T. Baldwin, M. Dras, J. Hockenmaier, T. H. King, and G. van Noord, editors, *Proceedings of the ACL 2007 Workshop on Deep Linguistic Processing*, pages 144–151, Prague, Czech Republic, June. Association for Computational Linguistics.

Amit Dubey and Frank Keller. 2003. Probabilistic parsing for german using sister-head dependencies. In *ACL*, pages 96–103.

Martin Forst. 2007. Filling statistics with linguistics – property design for the disambiguation of german lfg parses. In *ACL 2007 Workshop on Deep Linguistic Processing*, pages 17–24, Prague, Czech Republic, June. Association for Computational Linguistics.

Anette Frank, Hans-Ulrich Krieger, Feiyu Xu, Hans Uszkoreit, Berthold Crysmann, Brigitte Jörg, and Ulrich Schäfer. 2006. Querying structured knowledge sources. *Journal of Applied Logic*.

Tibor Kiss and Birgit Wesche. 1991. Verb order and head movement. In Otthein Herzog and Claus-Rolf Rollinger, editors, *Text Understanding in LILOG*, number 546 in Lecture Notes in Artificial Intelligence, pages 216–240. Springer-Verlag, Berlin.

Sandra Kübler, Erhard W. Hinrichs, and Wolfgang Maier. 2006. Is it really that difficult to parse german? In *Proceedings of EMNLP 2006, Sydney, Australia*.

Stefan Müller and Walter Kasper. 2000. HPSG analysis of German. In Wolfgang Wahlster, editor, *Verbmobil: Foundations of Speech-to-Speech Translation*, pages 238–253. Springer, Berlin.

Stephan Oepen, E. Callahan, Daniel Flickinger, Christopher Manning, and Kristina Toutanova. 2002. LinGO Redwoods: A rich and dynamic treebank for HPSG. In *Beyond PARSEVAL. Workshop at the Third International Conference on Language Resources and Evaluation, LREC 2002*, Las Palmas, Spain.

Stephan Oepen. 2002. *Competence and Performance Profiling for Constraint-based Grammars: A New Methodology, Toolkit, and Applications*. Ph.D. thesis, Saarland University.

Tobias Ruland. 2000. Probabilistic LR-parsing with symbolic postprocessing. In Wolfgang Wahlster, editor, *Verbmobil: Foundations of Speech-to-Speech Translation*, pages 147–162. Springer, Berlin.

Wojciech Skut, Thorsten Brants, and Hans Uszkoreit. 1998. A linguistically interpreted corpus of German newspaper text. In *Proceedings of the ESSLLI Workshop on Recent Advances in Corpus Annotation*, Saarbrücken, Germany.

Kristina Toutanova, Christopher D. Manning, Stuart M. Shieber, Dan Flickinger, and Stephan Oepen. 2002. Parse disambiguation for a rich HPSG grammar. In *Proceedings of the First Workshop on Treebanks and Linguistic Theories (TLT2002)*, pages 253–263, Sozopol, Bulgaria.

Hans Uszkoreit, Rolf Backofen, Stephan Busemann, Abdel Kader Diagne, Elizabeth Hinkelman, Walter Kasper, Bernd Kiefer, Hans-Ulrich Krieger, Klaus Netter, Günter Neumann, Stephan Oepen, and Stephen P. Spackman. 1994. Disco - an hpsg-based nlp system and its application for appointment scheduling. In *Proceedings of the 15th International Conference on Computational Linguistics (COLING'94), August 5-9*, volume 1, pages 436–440, Kyoto, Japan.

Wolfgang Wahlster, editor. 2000. *Verbmobil: Foundations of Speech-to-Speech Translation*. Springer, Berlin.

Part-of-Speech Tagging with a Symbolic Full Parser: Using the TIGER Treebank to Evaluate *Fips*

Yves Scherrer
Language Technology Laboratory (LATL)
University of Geneva
1211 Geneva 4, Switzerland
yves.scherrer@lettres.unige.ch

Abstract

In this paper, we introduce the German version of the multilingual *Fips* parsing system. We focus on the evaluation of its part-of-speech tagging component with the help of the TIGER treebank. We explain how *Fips* can be adapted to the tagset used by TIGER and report first results of this study: currently, 87% of words are tagged correctly. We also discuss some common errors and explore a possible extension of this study to parsing.

1 Introduction

Fips is a parsing framework based on the main assumptions of Chomsky's generative linguistics. It has been designed as a multilingual framework, making it easy to add new languages. Currently, it is available for six languages (English, French, German, Italian, Spanish and Greek). While the French version (providing the best coverage) has taken part in evaluation campaigns (Adda et al., 1998; Goldman et al., 2005), the other language modules have only been subject to internal qualitative evaluation. However, the availability of gold standard treebanks allows for quantitative evaluation of rule-based parsing systems. In particular, we propose to use the TIGER treebank for the evaluation of the German version of *Fips*.

This paper reports on research in progress. As a preliminary step towards a quantitative assessment of parser performance, we focus on the task of Part-of-Speech (POS) tag comparison here. This task is intended to yield a first appreciation of the quality of the German *Fips* component without having to deal with the full parser output and its possible incompatibilities due to underlying theoretical differences. Tag comparison operates on a word-by-word basis and provides binary measures of accuracy (tag identity or difference).

We extend our work to the tasks of lemma identification and morphological analysis: *Fips* as well as the TIGER treebank provide this information.

Fips has been developed independently of the TIGER treebank. Therefore, a large part of this paper deals with problems arising from mismatches between the design decisions made for *Fips* and the annotation guidelines of TIGER. In our view, a detailed discussion of these mismatches is essential for a fair assessment of the performances of *Fips*, but may also be interesting for future research involving evaluation.

This paper is organized as follows. In Section 2, we present the *Fips* framework. In Section 3, we recall the main characteristics of the TIGER treebank, explain the adaptations we applied to the *Fips* tagger and give some information about the evaluation setup. We go on to report the results for the three main tasks: Part-of-Speech tagging (Section 4), lemma identification (Section 5), and morphological analysis (Section 6). Section 7 compares our work to statistical POS tagging and to parser evaluation. We conclude by giving an overview of the benefits of quantitative evaluation.

2 The *Fips* framework

Fips (Wehrli, 2007) is a deep symbolic parser developed at the University of Geneva. It currently supports six languages, and others are under development. The parser is based on an adaption of generative linguistics, borrowing concepts from the Minimalist model (Chomsky, 1995), from the Simpler

Proceedings of the ACL-08: HLT Workshop on Parsing German (PaGe-08), pages 16–23,
Columbus, Ohio, USA, June 2008.

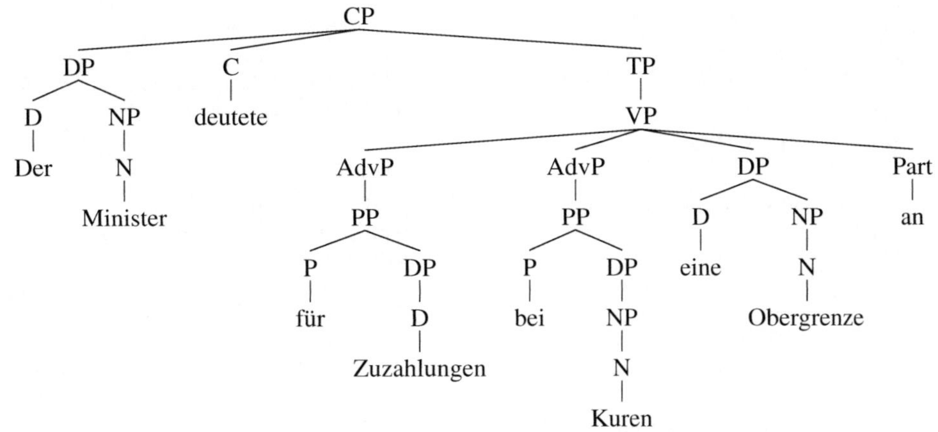

Figure 1: Example output of the German *Fips* parser.

Syntax model (Culicover and Jackendoff, 2005), as well as from Lexical Functional Grammar (Bresnan, 2001). Each syntactic constituent is represented as a simplified X-bar structure without intermediate levels, in the form $[_{XP} L X R]$. X denotes a lexical category, L and R stand for (possibly empty) lists of left and right subconstituents, respectively.

The originality of *Fips* lies in its two-layer architecture. Fundamental properties and structures that are common to all languages are defined in an abstract, language-independent layer. On a theoretical level, this layer can be associated to the concept of "universal grammar". On top of this layer, a particular, language-dependent layer extends the abstract structures and adds language-specific grammar rules. The *Fips* lexicon contains detailed morphosyntactic and semantic information such as selectional properties, subcategorization information and syntactico-semantic features. The parser is thus based on a strong lexicalist framework. In order to guide ambiguity resolution, numeric penalty values can be assigned to rules and lexemes.

The German component of *Fips* contains around 100 language-specific grammar rules. The lexicon contains 39 000 lexemes and 410 000 word forms. The word forms are generated by a rule-based morphological generator. The lexicon also contains 500 multi-word expressions and 1500 high-frequency compound nouns. Unknown compound nouns are chunked at runtime.

Fips operates in two modes: parser (see Figure 1) and tagger (see Figure 2) output.[1] The tagger output allows us to benefit from the rich information of the *Fips* lexicon, being at the same time more robust than the parser.

3 Experimental setup

3.1 The TIGER treebank

The TIGER treebank contains about 50 000 sentences of newspaper text, covering all domains (Brants et al., 2002). The annotation has been performed with the help of interactive tools. This methodology allows the human annotator to easily accept or reject proposals made by the computer. Part-of-speech tags are proposed by a statistical tagger trained on a manually annotated corpus. It uses the *Stuttgart-Tübingen-Tagset* (STTS) (Thielen et al., 1999). The parse trees were constructed interactively with the help of a statistical parser. Figure 3 shows an example of the TIGER export file.

3.2 Adaptations

In order to compare the *Fips* output with the TIGER tags, some adaptations had to be made. First of all, the tagset had to be changed to match the STTS tagset. While this procedure was straightforward for most of the categories, it showed that the German tagging module of *Fips* had never been subject

[1]The parser output is shown here for illustration – we do not use it in the present study.

Given the scope of this workshop, we forgo translating German examples into English.

der	ART	SIN-MAS-NOM	311000336	0	der	SUBJ
minister	NN	SIN-MAS-NOM	311019783	3	Minister	
deutete	VVFIN	IND-KON-PRA-3-SIN	311021998	12	andeuten	
für	APPR		311050006	20	für	
Zuzahlungen	NE	INN-ING-NOM-ACC-DAT	0	24	Zuzahlungen	
bei	APPR		311050009	36	bei	
kuren	NN	PLU-FEM-NOM-ACC-DAT-GEN	311004912	40	Kur	
eine	ART	SIN-FEM-NOM-ACC	311000346	46	ein	OBJ
ober¬	NN	SIN-MAS-NOM-ACC-DAT	311019956	51	Ober	COMP-CHUNK
grenze	NN	SIN-FEM-NOM-ACC	311001176	55	Grenze	COMP-HEAD
an	PTKVZ		311050018	62	an	
.	$.		0	65	.	

Figure 2: Example output of the German *Fips* tagger. The columns show: the word as found in the text; the POS tag in the STTS tagset; morphological information in a proprietary tagset; the lexeme number of the internal database (0 stands for unknown words); the character position at which the word begins; the lemma. The rightmost column contains additional information like grammatical function and compound noun syntax.
Note that the compound noun *Obergrenze* was automatically chunked and that the word *Zuzahlungen* was not found in the lexicon; the particle *an* is attached to the lemma of the main verb *deutete*.

to a rigorous evaluation. For example, there were no particular tags for pronominal prepositions (e.g., *darüber, deswegen*), for prepositions with articles (e.g., *beim, ins*), and for the infinitival particle *zu*.

Small adaptions concerned the replacement of *ß* by *ss* (*Fips* uses the Swiss Standard German orthography, lacking the letter *ß*) and the different lemmatization of the particle verbs: in TIGER and in contrast to *Fips*, the particles are not attached to the lemma (see the verb *andeuten* in Figures 2 and 3).

Finally, the *Fips* tagger contains a compound noun chunker which is automatically used for unknown words and which outputs one line for each chunk. These lines had to be reassembled to fit with the unchunked TIGER output (cf. the compound noun *Obergrenze* in Figures 2 and 3).

3.3 Evaluation

From the TIGER export file, we extracted the original sentences and submitted them to the *Fips* tagger. Then, we compared its results with the information given in TIGER. Overall, 792 885 words were compared. This number does not correspond to the 888 578 tokens of the TIGER corpus, because the concept of word is much more flexible in *Fips* than in TIGER. For example, the token *62jähriger* is split into two words *62* and *jähriger*. By contrast, *vor allem* is regarded as a single lexical item (adverb) by *Fips*, but as two words by TIGER. Moreover, for a currently unknown reason, some words do not show up in the output of the *Fips* tagger.

TIGER Tag	*Fips* Tag	Number	Percentage
NN	NE	12592	1.59
KON	ADV	8000	1.01
ADJD	ADV	6737	0.85
ADV	PTKA	4976	0.63
NE	NN	4782	0.60
VAFIN	VVFIN	3529	0.45
ART	PRELS	2935	0.37
VVFIN	VVIMP	1937	0.24
VVINF	VVFIN	1859	0.23
VVPP	VVFIN	1624	0.20
Correct tags		692 386	87.32
Tested words		792 885	100.00

Table 1: Results of the part-of-speech tag comparison. The table shows the number of tags correctly predicted by *Fips* (second last line), as well as the ten most frequent erroneous predictions. The first column shows the correct tag as given by TIGER, the second column shows the erroneous tag assigned by *Fips*.

4 Part-of-speech tagging results

The most important part of this evaluation concerns the part-of-speech tags. As explained above, we have adapted *Fips* to generate STTS tags. Table 1 shows the number of correctly predicted tags, and the ten most frequent tagging errors. In the following sections, we discuss some of these errors.

4.1 Proper and common nouns

The most common error is related to the distinction between proper (NE) and common nouns (NN). This error affects 2.19% of words (see first and fifth line in Table 1) and accounts for 17.29% of all tagging errors. Currently, the distinction between proper and common nouns is implemented in *Fips* as follows.

A noun is regarded as common noun if:

- it is present in the lexicon and not explicitly marked as proper noun: *Chemie, Hirsch, Konkurrenz*, or
- it is a compound noun that can be analyzed into chunks which are present in the lexicon: *Bundes+bank, Finanz+markt, Sitz+platz.*

A noun is regarded as proper noun if:

- it is explicitly marked as such in the lexicon: *Gregor, Berlin, Europa.*
- it is not present in the lexicon and cannot be fully analyzed as compound noun: *Talk, Gaullismus, Kibbuzarbeiter.*

Tagging errors occur in two ways. Words that are annotated as common nouns by TIGER are annotated as proper nouns by *Fips* (see first line in Table 1). This happens for all common nouns that are not present in the lexicon (e.g., *Primadonna, Portfolio, Niedersachse, Gaullismus*). There are also compound nouns with a proper noun complement: *Vichy-Zeiten, Spreearm.* While TIGER considers these words as common nouns because the head is a common noun, *Fips* still analyzes them as proper nouns. For other words like *Marseillaise*, the TIGER annotation as common noun may be questioned.

In the other way, some TIGER proper nouns have been tagged by *Fips* as common nouns (cf. fifth line in Table 1). One common category of erroneous tagging is the case of homonymous proper and common nouns. For example, *Kohl* and *Teufel* are common nouns, but also the names of German politicians and therefore proper nouns. These misinterpretations are due to the fact that *Fips* does not contain any specific Named Entity Recognition module. While *Fips* successfully relies on letter case to identify proper nouns in other languages, this approach obviously does not work in German.

Some proper nouns exhibit a more subtle phenomenon: words like *Mannheim, Wendland* or *Kantstrasse* are analyzed by *Fips* as common compound nouns (*Mann+Heim, wenden+Land, Kante+Strasse*). Again, a Named Entity Recognition system would prevent such unfortunate analyses. Furthermore, we do not find it compelling to analyze *Buddha, Bundesbank* and *Bundeskriminalamt* as proper nouns.

To sum up, the source of noun mistagging is threefold. First, the *Fips* lexicon contains some gaps. Second, the lack of a Named Entity Recognition module in *Fips* causes an overgeneration of homograph common nouns where a proper noun would be appropriate. Third, the distinction between proper and common nouns is not clear-cut, and some divergences can be considered as normal.

4.2 Conjunctions and adverbs

Conjunctions are frequently mistagged as adverbs. Above all, this error affects the words *und, aber, denn*, which can have an adverbial (ADV) or a conjunction (KON) reading. In (1), the first occurrence of *und* is erroneously tagged as adverb. However, if we parse the first part of the sentence only (2), *Fips* obtains the correct conjunction reading. This suggests that the conjunction reading is available also for (1), but that the ranking mechanism is flawed and prefers the adverb reading.

(1) Automaten sind dort nur in Geschäften und Restaurants erlaubt und nicht wie in der Bundesrepublik auch im Freien.

(2) Automaten sind dort nur in Geschäften und Restaurants erlaubt.

In general, it seems that *Fips* gets the conjunctions right in short sentences, while it easily gets confused with longer sentences. However, the preference for the adverbial reading can be easily explained. In order to propose a conjunction, the parser must identify two conjuncts of the same category, whereas an adverb does not have that requirement. Thus, if the parser fails to find two suitable conjuncts, it will propose the less constrained adverbial reading.

#BOS 47149 0 1088427994 0					
Der	der	ART	Nom.Sg.Masc	NK	500
Minister	Minister	NN	Nom.Sg.Masc	NK	500
deutete	deuten	VVFIN	3.Sg.Past.Ind	HD	504
für	für	APPR	–	AC	503
Zuzahlungen	Zuzahlung	NN	Acc.Pl.Fem	NK	503
bei	bei	APPR	–	AC	501
Kuren	Kur	NN	Dat.Pl.Fem	NK	501
eine	ein	ART	Acc.Sg.Fem	NK	502
Obergrenze	Obergrenze	NN	Acc.Sg.Fem	NK	502
an	an	PTKVZ	–	SVP	504
.	–	$.	–	–	0
#500	–	NP	–	SB	504
#501	–	PP	–	MNR	503
#502	–	NP	–	OA	504
#503	–	PP	–	MO	504
#504	–	S	–	–	0
#EOS 47149					

Figure 3: An example sentence of the TIGER corpus. The *#BOS* and *#EOS* lines mark the beginning and the end of a sentence. The columns show: the word (or word component) as found in the text; the lemma; the POS tag in the STTS tagset; the morphological features. The fifth and sixth column, as well as the lines beginning with *#50x*, contain information for the construction of the parse tree and are not relevant for our study.

4.3 Adjectives and adverbs

In contrast to English or French, there is no formal difference in German between adjectives used as predicates (e.g., *Er ist schnell*) or as adverbs (e.g., *Er fährt schnell*). This formal identity may have motivated the developers of the STTS tagset to use the same tag (ADJD) in both cases. In contrast, the German *Fips* tagger is based on earlier work on French and English, where distinct tags for adverbials and predicatives are needed. Therefore, it also uses different tags for German.

We tried to come up with a simple solution to this problem by assigning the ADJD tag to all adverbs whose base forms are homograph with an adjective. However, in this case, we also assigned the ADJD tag to words like *ganz, natürlich, wirklich*, which are tagged as proper adverbs (ADV) in TIGER. In short, we had the choice of either overgenerating ADV tags (keeping the *Fips* output as-is) or overgenerating ADJD tags (with the homograph modification). Preliminary tests showed similar amounts of overgeneration in both cases. We have thus chosen to stick to the original *Fips* analyses.

4.4 Particles followed by adjectives

STTS introduces a special tag (PTKA) for particles "followed by adjectives or adverbs", for example *am [schönsten], zu [schnell]*. In *Fips*, the class of comparative adverbs also contains *auch, so* and *mehr*. Of course, these words are not always followed by adjectives, and should thus not always be given the PTKA tag. While different readings are indeed available in the *Fips* lexicon, the results suggest that *Fips* overgeneralizes the comparative reading and assigns the PTKA tag even in cases where a normal ADV tag would be adequate. (3) shows a sentence where *Fips* erroneously assigned the PTKA tag to *auch*.

(3) Der Verkehrssenator, wie er künftig auch heißen möge, …

4.5 Pronouns

The seventh line refers to the homography of the definite determiner and the relative pronoun (PRELS) whenever *Fips* cannot find an agreement between the determiner and the head of the noun phrase.

(4) Neue Debatte über den Atomschild

In (4), the *Fips* lexicon only contains the neuter lexeme *Schild* (which serves as a head of the compound noun *Atomschild*), but not the rarer masculine homograph lexeme. This lexical gap prevents the masculine determiner *den* to be attached to *Atomschild* as a determiner, and *Fips* resorts to the relative pronoun analysis instead.

4.6 Verb problems

Verb tagging seems to be a serious problem to *Fips*: four of the ten most frequent tagging errors involve verbs.

The first type of error is related to the distinction between auxiliary and full verbs. The three auxiliary verbs *haben, sein, werden* can also have full verb readings, depending on the context. We recently observed that *Fips* preferred the auxiliary reading even in cases where a full verb reading is required, and subsequently modified the constraints on the lexeme selection. It now turns out that these constraints are too strong and lead to a massive overgeneration of the full verb reading.

Then, *Fips* tends to overgenerate imperatives: third person singular forms are erroneously analyzed as imperative plurals (e.g., *kommt, schreit*). Again, this is due to agreement constraints: the third person singular requires an overt subject, while an imperative does not. If *Fips* fails to find a subject that agrees with the verb (for example because of an undetected long distance dependency), it will resort to an imperative reading. In the future development of *Fips*, further restrictions should be imposed on the use of imperative forms as these are extremely rare in newspaper text.

The last two lines in Table 1 reveal that finite verb forms are preferred to infinite forms: infinitives are mistagged as finite plural forms, and past participles without *ge-* prefix are mistagged as third person singular forms (for regular verbs) or as past plural form (for irregular verbs with *-en* participle). These phenomena depend on long distance relations and should typically benefit from a full parsing approach like the one used by *Fips*. Two factors may explain why this is not the case. First, many sentences in which such errors occur could not be parsed completely by *Fips*; long distance relations are not fully detected in these cases. Second, the implementation of passive and modal sentences is incomplete and lacks some essential constraints on verb form selection.

TIGER Base Form	*Fips* Base Form
dieser	diese
anderer	ander
welche	welcher
Beamte	Beamter
Angestellte	Angestellter

Figure 4: For some pronouns and nouns, TIGER and *Fips* use different base forms.

5 Lemmatizer results

On the whole TIGER corpus (792 885 words), 94.32% of the words (747 855) were correctly lemmatized. Most errors were due to diverging base form choices. This especially holds for pronouns and nominalized adjectives (cf. Figure 4), but also for pronouns. In TIGER, feminine and neuter pronouns always refer to the masculine lemma, whereas *Fips* separates the genders more strictly: *der (Dat.Sg.Fem)* refers to the lemma *der (Nom.Sg.Masc)* in TIGER, but to *die (Nom.Sg.Fem)* in *Fips*. Moreover, participles used as adjectives keep the infinitive as base form in *Fips*, but not in TIGER.

Some lemma errors are due to wrong POS tagging. For instance, we found that *Fips* overgenerates imperatives. For example, *einig* is not analyzed as adjective, but as the imperative singular (with elision of final e) of *sich einigen*; the adjective *nötige* is analyzed as the imperative singular of *nötigen*. However, such awkward analyses should be easy to iron out.

Globally, we find that very few errors are directly due to the lemmatizer; most of them are either due to different base forms or to POS tagging errors.

6 Morphology results

After the discussion of the part-of-speech tagger and lemmatizer functionalities of *Fips*, we now turn to the last functionality, the morphological analyzer. We restricted our evaluation to the words that obtained correct POS tags: if the POS tag is already wrong, it is very likely that the morphology will be wrong as well. Table 2 reports the results of the mor-

Type	Number	Percentage
Number mismatch	15617	2.26
Case mismatch	12420	1.79
Gender mismatch	8461	1.22
Degree mismatch	514	0.07
Person mismatch	108	0.02
Correct analysis or no morphology	665 110	96.06
Tested words	692 386	100.00

Table 2: Results of the morphological analysis. The table presents the numbers of words that have been correctly analyzed by *Fips*, and the types of errors that occurred. A word can present several mismatch types.

phology evaluation. Parts of speech without inflection were considered as correctly analyzed. We split the errors into five categories, according to the inflection feature that *Fips* failed to predict correctly. The different mismatch types do not sum up to 100% because a word can show several mismatches (e.g., a noun can show case and number mismatch), and because not all types of mismatch apply to all parts of speech (for instance, degree mismatch only applies to adjectives).

It is not easy to find recurrent patterns in the errors. However, we found that most errors occurred in noun phrases. Most inflected adjective and article forms admit several morphological analyses, but the ambiguities can usually be reduced by the syntactic context. If the ambiguities are reduced in an incorrect way, this means that the syntactic context has been analyzed badly. In other words, such morphology errors often reflect bad parses. Therefore, it might be useful to address these errors before evaluating the parsing performance of *Fips*. Another rather odd fact is that nouns with identical singular and plural forms (for example, *Minister, Unternehmen*) prefer to be analyzed as plurals by *Fips*. Here again, these cases hint at bad parses.

Degree mismatches result from a bug in *Fips*: comparative forms in predicative positions as in (5) are assigned the positive tag instead of the comparative one.

(5) . . . um noch *tiefer* in den Kosmos blicken zu können.

7 Related work

It may be interesting to compare *Fips* to a statistical part-of-speech tagger for German. The TnT tagger (Brants, 2000) is based on Hidden Markov Models, and has been trained and tested on the NEGRA corpus (Skut et al., 1997); NEGRA is the predecessor of TIGER and uses the same tagset. Brants (2000) reports an overall accuracy of 96.7%. However, TnT is not directly comparable to *Fips* for several reasons.

First, we showed that *Fips* originally used a different tagset, based on different linguistic assumptions than STTS. Those conceptional differences make up a large part of the errors, as has been shown for the distinction between the ADJD and ADV tags. By contrast, TnT has been trained directly over the STTS tagset and should thus not present such errors.

Second, the recurrence of certain error patterns with *Fips* illustrates the classical problem of manual rule ranking and weighting in rule-based systems.

Third, *Fips* has been conceived as a parser in the first place, and its tagger functionality should rather be viewed as a by-product. Hence, its algorithms are not optimized for POS tagging. While there may be simpler approaches to obtain high tagging accuracy, the method chosen for *Fips* seems theoretically more plausible to us.

As we pointed out at the beginning, this tagger evaluation has been started as a first step towards the evaluation of the *Fips* parser. While POS tagging has the advantage of operating word-by-word and of being rather theory-independent, these two properties do not hold for parsing.

The phrase trees in TIGER are rather flat, while the ones generated by *Fips* are deeper and closer to recent generative grammar frameworks. We will thus need to define the type of constituents that can be compared. An even bigger issue is the allowance of discontinuous phrases and crossing branches in TIGER, whereas *Fips* resolves these phenomena by resorting to projections and traces. Further research has to show if these structural differences can be overcome in order to lead to a meaningful comparison. The exact evaluation metric will also have to be chosen. While PARSEVAL (Black et al., 1991) is still one of the most important metrics, other measures may be more adapted to our problem (Carroll et al., 2002; Rehbein and van Genabith, 2007).

8 Conclusion

As we remarked above, this article reports on work in progress. Until now, we have been able to show that the general approach of evaluating *Fips* with the help of the TIGER treebank is valid. With very little adaptation work (see Section 3.2), we managed to obtain 87.32% of POS-tagging accuracy. This is a very promising beginning, and the discussion of the errors has shown that there are many "low hanging fruits" to improve the performance.

In any way, we find that the quantitative evaluation of NLP systems can be quite rewarding: developing rule-based systems is a complex task, often guided by vague intuitions about parsing quality. Quantitative evaluation allows us to measure the progress of the development and guarantees us that improvements on one parameter do not yield unwanted side effects on another.

Finally, the quantitative evaluation of the POS tagging performances yields important feedback on the forces and weaknesses of *Fips*. The result of the evaluation can be viewed as a sort of priority list for the developer. By working on the most common errors in a target-oriented way, (s)he is guaranteed to invest his/her time in a maximally effective manner. Such guiding principles are very valuable for the further development of any rule-based parsing system, independently of the precise accuracy figures of the evaluation. Even if the adaptation of two different tagsets and tagging philosophies is not straightforward, we plan to extend our evaluation to other languages of the *Fips* project for which suitable gold standard corpora exist.

Acknowledgements

We thank Eric Wehrli and for his precious support for this work and for his valuable comments on previous versions of this paper.

References

G. Adda, J. Mariani, J. Lecomte, P. Paroubek, and M. Rajman. 1998. The GRACE French part-of-speech tagging evaluation task. In *Proceedings of the First International Conference on Language Resources and Evaluation (LREC)*, Granada.

E. Black, S. Abney, S. Flickenger, C. Gdaniec, C. Grishman, P. Harrison, D. Hindle, R. Ingria, F. Jelinek, J. Klavans, M. Liberman, M. Marcus, S. Roukos, B. Santorini, and T. Strzalkowski. 1991. Procedure for quantitatively comparing the syntactic coverage of English grammars. In *HLT '91: Proceedings of the Workshop on Speech and Natural Language*, pages 306–311, Pacific Grove, California.

S. Brants, S. Dipper, S. Hansen, W. Lezius, and G. Smith. 2002. The TIGER Treebank. In *Proceedings of the Workshop on Treebanks and Linguistic Theories*, Sozopol.

T. Brants. 2000. TnT – a statistical part-of-speech tagger. In *Proceedings of the Sixth Applied Natural Language Processing (ANLP-2000)*, Seattle.

J. Bresnan. 2001. *Lexical Functional Syntax*. Blackwell, Oxford.

J. Carroll, A. Frank, D. Lin, D. Prescher, and H. Uszkoreit. 2002. Beyond PARSEVAL – towards improved evaluation measures for parsing systems. In *Proceedings of the LREC 2002 Workshop*, Las Palmas, Gran Canaria.

N. Chomsky. 1995. *The Minimalist Program*. MIT Press, Cambridge, Mass.

P. W. Culicover and R. Jackendoff. 2005. *Simpler Syntax*. Oxford University Press, Oxford.

J.-P. Goldman, C. Laenzlinger, G. Soare, and E. Wehrli. 2005. L'analyseur syntaxique multilingue Fips dans la campagne EASy. In *Proceedings of TALN XII*, volume 2, pages 35–49, Dourdan.

I. Rehbein and J. van Genabith. 2007. Treebank annotation schemes and parser evaluation for German. In *Proceedings of the 2007 Joint Conference on Empirical Methods in Natural Language Processing and Computational Natural Language Learning (EMNLP/CoNLL 2007)*, pages 630–639, Prague.

W. Skut, B. Krenn, T. Brants, and H. Uszkoreit. 1997. An annotation scheme for free word order languages. In *Proceedings of the Fifth Conference on Applied Natural Language Processing ANLP-97*, Washington, DC.

C. Thielen, A. Schiller, S. Teufel, and C. Stöckert. 1999. Guidelines für das Tagging deutscher Textkorpora mit STTS. Technical report, University of Stuttgart and University of Tübingen.

E. Wehrli. 2007. Fips, a "deep" linguistic multilingual parser. In *Proceedings of the ACL 2007 Workshop on Deep Linguistic Processing*, pages 120–127, Prague.

Revisiting the impact of different annotation schemes on PCFG parsing: A grammatical dependency evaluation

Adriane Boyd
Department of Linguistics
The Ohio State University
1712 Neil Avenue
Columbus, Ohio 43210, USA
adriane@ling.osu.edu

Detmar Meurers
Seminar für Sprachwissenschaft
Universität Tübingen
Wilhelmstrasse 19
72074 Tübingen, Germany
dm@sfs.uni-tuebingen.de

Abstract

Recent parsing research has started addressing the questions a) how parsers trained on different syntactic resources differ in their performance and b) how to conduct a meaningful evaluation of the parsing results across such a range of syntactic representations. Two German treebanks, Negra and TüBa-D/Z, constitute an interesting testing ground for such research given that the two treebanks make very different representational choices for this language, which also is of general interest given that German is situated between the extremes of fixed and free word order. We show that previous work comparing PCFG parsing with these two treebanks employed PARSEVAL and grammatical function comparisons which were skewed by differences between the two corpus annotation schemes. Focusing on the grammatical dependency triples as an essential dimension of comparison, we show that the two very distinct corpora result in comparable parsing performance.

1 Introduction

Syntactically annotated corpora have been produced for a range of languages and they differ significantly regarding which language properties are encoded and how they are represented. Between the two extremes of constituency treebanks for English and dependency treebanks for free word order languages such as Czech lie languages such as German, for which two different treebanks have explored different options for encoding topology and dependency, Negra (Brants et al., 1999) and TüBa-D/Z (Telljohann et al., 2005).

Recent research has started addressing the question of how parsers trained on these different syntactic resources differ in their performance. Such work must also address the question of how to conduct a meaningful evaluation of the parsing results across such a range of syntactic representations. In this paper, we show that previous work comparing PCFG parsing for the two German treebanks used representations which cannot adequately be compared using the given PARSEVAL measures and that a grammatical dependency evaluation is more meaningful than the grammatical function evaluation provided.

We present the first comparison of Negra and TüBa-D/Z using a labeled dependency evaluation based on the grammatical function labels provided in the corpora. We show that, in contrast to previous literature, a labeled dependency evaluation establishes that PCFG parsers trained on the two corpora give similar parsing performance. The focus on labeled dependencies also provides a direct link to recent work on dependency-based evaluation (e.g., Clark and Curran, 2007) and dependency parsing (e.g., CoNLL shared tasks 2006, 2007).

1.1 Previous work

The question of how to evaluate parser output has naturally already arisen in earlier work on parsing English. As discussed by Lin (1995) and others, the PARSEVAL evaluation typically used to analyze the performance of statistical parsing models has many drawbacks. Bracketing evaluation may count a single error multiple times and does not differentiate between errors that significantly affect the interpretation of the sentence and those that are less crucial.

Proceedings of the ACL-08: HLT Workshop on Parsing German (PaGe-08), pages 24–32,
Columbus, Ohio, USA, June 2008.

It also does not allow for evaluation of particular syntactic structures or provide meaningful information about where the parser is failing. In addition, and most directly relevant for this paper, PARSEVAL scores are difficult to compare across syntactic annotation schemes (Carroll et al., 2003).

At the same time, previous research on PCFG parsing using treebank training data present PARSEVAL measures in comparing the parsing performance for different languages and annotation schemes, reporting a number of striking differences. For example, Levy and Manning (2003), Kübler (2005), and Kübler et al. (2006) highlight the significant effect of language properties and annotation schemes for German and Chinese treebanks. In related work, parser enhancements that provide a significant performance boost for English, such as head lexicalization, are reported not to provide the same kind of improvement, if any, for German (Dubey and Keller, 2003; Dubey, 2004; Kübler et al., 2006).

Previous work has compared the similar Negra and Tiger corpora of German to the very different TüBa-D/Z corpus. Kübler et al. (2006) compares the Negra and TüBa-D/Z corpora of German using a PARSEVAL evaluation and an evaluation on core grammatical function labels that is included to address concerns about the PARSEVAL measure.[1] Using the Stanford Parser (Klein and Manning, 2002), which employs a factored PCFG and dependency model, they claim that the model trained on TüBa-D/Z consistently outperforms that trained on Negra in PARSEVAL and grammatical function evaluations. Dubey (2004) also includes an evaluation on grammatical function for statistical models trained on Negra, but obtains very different results from Kübler et al. (2006).[2]

In recent related work, Rehbein and van Genabith (2007a) demonstrate using the Tiger and TüBa-D/Z corpora of German that PARSEVAL is inappropriate for comparisons of the output of PCFG parsers trained on different treebank annotation schemes because PARSEVAL scores are affected by the ratio of terminal to non-terminal nodes. A dependency-based evaluation on triples of the form *word-POS-head* shows better results for the parser trained on Tiger even though the much lower PARSEVAL scores, if meaningful, would predict that the output for Tiger is of lower quality. However, their dependency-based evaluation does not make use of the grammatical function labels, which are provided in the corpora and closely correspond to the representations used in recent work on formalism-independent evaluation of parsers (e.g., Clark and Curran, 2007).[3]

Addressing these issues, we resolve the apparent discrepancy between Kübler et al. (2006) and Dubey (2004) and establish a firm grammatical function comparison of Negra and TüBa-D/Z. We also extend the evaluation to a labeled dependency evaluation based on grammatical relations for both corpora. Such an evaluation, which abstracts away from the specifics of the annotation schemes, shows that, in contrast to the claims made in Kübler et al. (2006), the parsing results for PCFG parsers trained on these heterogeneous corpora are very similar.

2 The corpora used

As motivated in the introduction, the work discussed in this paper is based on two German corpora, Negra and TüBa-D/Z, which differ significantly in the syntactic representations used – thereby offering an interesting test bed for investigating the influence of an annotation scheme on the parsers trained.

2.1 Negra

The Negra corpus (Brants et al., 1999) consists of newspaper text from the *Frankfurter Rundschau*, a German newspaper. Version 2 of the corpus contains 20,602 sentences. It uses the STTS tag set (Schiller et al., 1995) for part-of-speech annotation. There are 25 non-terminal node labels and 46 edge labels.

The syntactic annotation of Negra combines features from phrase structure grammar and depen-

[1]The evaluation is based only on the grammatical function; it does not identify the dependency pair that it labels.

[2]While the focus of Kübler et al. (2006) is on comparing parsing results across corpora, Dubey (2004) focuses on improving parsing for Negra, including corpus-specific enhancements leading to better results. This difference in focus and additional differences in experimental setup mean that a fine-grained comparison of the results is inappropriate – the relevant point here is that the gap between the results (23% for subjects, 35% for accusative objects) warrants further attention in the context of comparing parsing results across corpora.

[3]Their evaluation also introduces an additional level of complexity by finding heads heuristically rather than relying on the head labels present on some elements in each corpus.

dency grammar using a tree-like syntactic structure with grammatical functions labeled on the edges of the tree. Flat sentence structures are used in many places to avoid attachment ambiguities and non-branching phrases are not used.

The annotation scheme emphasizes the use of the tree structure to encode grammatical dependencies, representing a head and all its dependents within a local tree regardless of whether a dependent is realized near its head or not, e.g., because it has been extraposed or fronted. Since traditional syntax trees do not permit the crossing branches needed to license discontinuous constituents, Negra uses a "syntax graph" data structure to represent the annotation. An example of a syntax graph with a discontinuous constituent (VP) due to a fronted dative object (NP) is shown in Figure 1.

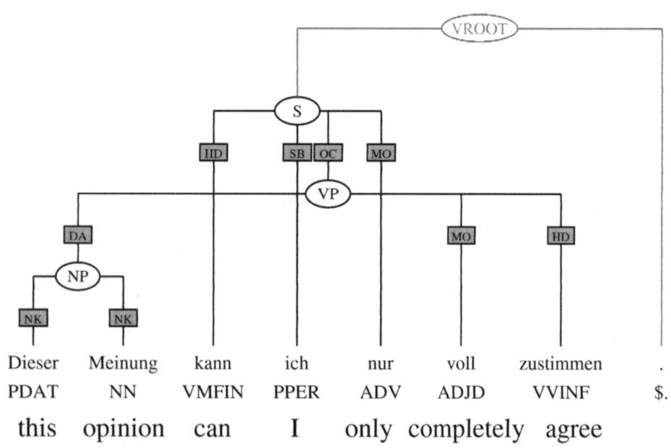

Figure 1: Negra tree for *'I can only agree with this opinion completely.'*

Negra uses flat NP and PP annotation with no marked heads. For example, both *Dieser* and *Meinung* in Figure 1 have the grammatical function label "NK". Since unary branching is not used in Negra, a bare noun or pronoun argument is not dominated by an NP node, as shown by the pronoun *ich* above.

A verbal head in Negra is always marked with the edge label "HD" and its arguments are its sisters in the local tree. The subject is always the sister of the finite verb, which is a daughter of S. If the finite verb is the main verb in the clause, the objects are also its sisters, i.e., the finite verb, subject and objects are all daughters of S. If the main verb is an auxiliary governing a non-finite main verb, the non-finite verb and its objects and modifiers form a VP where the objects are sisters of the non-finite verb as in Figure 1. The VP is then a sister of the finite verb.

The finite verb in a German declarative clause appears in the so-called verb-second position, immediately following the fronted constituent. As a result, the VP in Negra is discontinuous whenever one of its children has been fronted, as in the common word orders exemplified in (1a) and (1b).

(1) a. **Die Tür** hat Anna **wieder zugeschlagen**.
the door has Anna again slammed-shut
'Anna slammed the door shut again.'

b. **Wieder** hat Anna **die Tür zugeschlagen**.
again has Anna the door slammed-shut
'Anna slammed the door shut again.'

The sentence we saw in Figure 1 contains a discontinuous VP with a fronted dative object (*Dieser Meinung*). The dative object and a modifier (*voll*) form a VP with the non-finite verb (*zustimmen*).

2.2 TüBa-D/Z

The TüBa-D/Z corpus, version 2, (Telljohann et al., 2005) consists of 22,091 sentences of newspaper text from the German newspaper *die tageszeitung*. Like Negra, it uses the STTS tag set (Schiller et al., 1995) for part-of-speech annotation. Syntactically it uses 27 non-terminal node labels and 47 edge labels.

The syntactic annotation incorporates a topological field analysis of the German clause (Reis, 1980; Höhle, 1986), which segments a sentence into topological units depending on the position of the finite verb (verb-first, verb-second, verb-last). In a verb-first and verb-second sentence, the finite verb is the left bracket (LK), whereas in a verb-last subordinate clause, the subordinating conjunction occupies that field. In all clauses, the non-finite verb cluster forms the right bracket (VC), and arguments and modifiers can appear in the middle field (MF) between the two brackets. Extraposed material is found to the right of the right bracket, and in a verb-second sentence one constituent appears in the fronted field (VF) preceding the finite verb. By specifying constraints on the elements that can occur in the different fields, the word order in any type of German clause can be concisely characterized.

Each clause in the TüBa-D/Z corpus is divided into topological fields at the top level, and each topological field contains phrase-level annotation. An example sentence from TüBa-D/Z is shown in Figure 2, where the topological fields VF, LK, MF, and VC are visible under the SIMPX clause node.

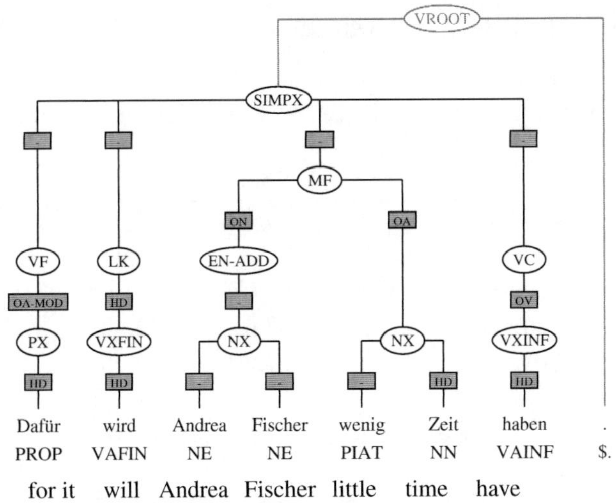

Figure 2: TüBa-D/Z tree for *'Andrea Fischer will have little time for it.'*

Edge labels are used to mark heads and grammatical functions, even though it can be nontrivial to figure out which grammatical function belongs to which head given that heads and their arguments often are in separate topological fields. For example, in Figure 2 the subject noun chunk (NX) has the edge label ON (object - nominative) and the object noun chunk has the edge label OA (object - accusative); both are realized within the middle field (MF), while the finite verb (VXFIN) marked as HD (head) is in the left sentence bracket (LK). This issue becomes relevant in section 3.4.2, discussing an evaluation based on labeled dependency triples.

Where Negra uses discontinuous constituents, TüBa-D/Z uses special edge labels to annotate grammatical relations which are not locally realized. For example, the fronted prepositional phrase (PX) in Figure 2 has the edge label OA-MOD which needs to be matched with the noun phrase (NX) with label OA that is found in the MF field.

2.3 Comparing Negra and TüBa-D/Z

To give an impression of how the different annotation schemes affect the appearance of a typical tree in the two corpora, Table 1 provides statistics on average sentence length and the number of nonterminals per sentence.

	Negra	TüBa-D/Z
No. of Sentences	20,602	22,091
Terminals/Sentence	17.2	17.3
Non-terminals/Sentence	7.0	20.7

Table 1: General Characteristics of the Corpora

While the sentences in Negra and TüBa-D/Z on average have the same number of words, the average TüBa-D/Z sentence has nearly three times as many non-terminal nodes as the average Negra sentence. This difference is mainly due to the extra level of topological fields annotation and the use of more contoured structures in many places where Negra uses flatter structures.

3 Experiments

The goal of the following experiments is a comparison of parsing performance across different types of evaluation metrics for parsers trained on Negra (Ver. 2) and TüBa-D/Z (Ver. 2).

3.1 Data Preparation

Following Kübler et al. (2006), only sentences with fewer than 35 words were used, which results in 20,002 sentences for Negra and 21,365 sentences for TüBa-D/Z. Because punctuation is not attached within the sentence in the corpus annotation, punctuation was removed.

To be able to train PCFG parsing models, it is necessary to convert the syntax graphs encoding trees with discontinuities in Negra into traditional syntax trees. Around 30% of sentences in Negra contain at least one discontinuity. To remove discontinuities, we used the conversion program included with the Negra corpus annotation tools (Brants and Plaehn, 2000), the same tool used in Kübler et al. (2006), which raises non-head elements to a higher tree until there are no more discontinuities. For example, for the discontinuous tree with a fronted object we saw in Figure 1, the PP containing the fronted NP *Dieser Meinung* is raised to become a daughter of the top S node.[4]

Additionally, the edge labels used in both corpora need to be folded into the node labels to become a

[4]An alternate method that avoids certain problems with this raising method is discussed in Boyd (2007).

part of context-free grammar rules used by a PCFG parser. In the Penn Treebank-style versions of the corpora appropriate for training a PCFG parser, each edge label is joined with the phrase or POS label on the phrase or word immediately below it. Both corpora include edge labels above all phrases and words. However the flatter structures in Negra result in 39 different edge labels on words while TüBa-D/Z has only 5.

Unlike Kübler et al. (2006), which ignored edge labels on words, we incorporate all edge labels present in both corpora. As a consequence of this, providing a parser with perfect lexical tags would also provide the edge label for that word. TüBa-D/Z does not annotate grammatical functions other than HD on words, but Negra includes many grammatical functions on words. Including edge labels in the perfect lexical tags would artificially boost the results of a grammatical function evaluation for Negra since it amounts to providing the correct grammatical function for the 38% of arguments in Negra that are single words.

To avoid this problem, we introduced non-branching phrasal nodes into Negra to prevent the correct grammatical function label from being provided with the perfect lexical tag in the cases of single-word arguments, which are mostly bare nouns and pronouns. We added phrasal nodes above all single-word subject, accusative object, dative object, and genitive object[5] arguments, with the category of the inserted phrase depending on the POS tag on the word. The introduced phrasal node is given the word's original grammatical function label; the grammatical function label of the word itself becomes NK for NPs and HD for APs and VPs. In total, 14,580 nodes were inserted into Negra in this way. TüBa-D/Z has non-branching phrases above all single-word arguments, so that no such modification was needed.[6]

3.2 Experimental Setup

We trained unlexicalized PCFG parsing models using LoPar (Schmid, 2000). Unlexicalized models were used to minimize the impact of other corpus differences on parsing. A ten-fold cross validation was performed for all experiments.[7]

3.3 PARSEVAL Evaluation

As a reference point for comparison with previous work, the PARSEVAL results[8] are given in Table 2.

	Negra	TüBa-D/Z
Unlabeled Precision	78.69	89.92
Unlabeled Recall	82.29	86.48
Labeled Precision	64.08	75.36
Labeled Recall	67.01	72.47
Coverage	97.00	99.90

Table 2: PARSEVAL Evaluation

The parser trained on TüBa-D/Z performs much better than the one trained on Negra on all labeled and unlabeled bracketing scores. As we saw in section 2, Negra and TüBa-D/Z use very different syntactic annotation schemes, resulting in over 2.5 times as many non-terminals per sentence in TüBa-D/Z as in Negra with the additional unary nodes. As mentioned previously, Rehbein and van Genabith (2007a) showed that PARSEVAL is affected by the ratio of terminal to non-terminal nodes, so these results are not expected to indicate the quality of the parses. The comparison with grammatical function and dependency evaluations we turn to next showcases that PARSEVAL does not provide a meaningful evaluation metric across annotation schemes.

3.4 Dependency Evaluation

Complementing the issue of the ratio of terminals to non-terminals raised in the last section, one can question whether counting all brackets in the sentence equally, as done by the PARSEVAL metric, provides a good measure of how accurately the basic functor-argument structure of the sentence has been captured in a parse. Thus, it is useful to per-

[5] Genitive objects are modified for the sake of consistency among arguments even though there are too few genitive objects to provide reliable results in the evaluation.

[6] The addition of edge labels to terminal POS labels results in 337 lexical tags for Negra and 91 for TüBa-D/Z.

[7] Our experimental setup is designed to support a comparison between Negra and TüBa-D/Z for the three evaluation metrics and is intended to be comparable to the setup of Kübler et al. (2006). For Negra, Dubey (2004) explores a range of parsing models and the corpus preparation he uses differs from the one discussed in this paper so that a discussion of his results is beyond the scope of the corpus comparison in this paper.

[8] Scores were calculated using `evalb`.

form an evaluation based on the grammatical function labels that are important for determining the functor-argument structure of the sentence: subjects, accusative objects, and dative objects.[9] The first step in an evaluation of functor-argument structure is to identify whether an argument bears the correct grammatical function label.

3.4.1 Grammatical Function Label Evaluation

Kübler et al. (2006) present the results shown in Table 3 for the parsing performance of the unlexicalized model of the Stanford Parser (Klein and Manning, 2002). In this grammatical function label evaluation, TüBa-D/Z outperforms Negra for subjects, accusative objects, and dative objects based on an evaluation of phrasal arguments.

	Negra			TüBa-D/Z		
	Prec	Rec	F	Prec	Rec	F
Subj	52.50	58.02	55.26	66.82	75.93	72.38
Acc	35.14	36.30	35.72	43.84	47.31	45.58
Dat	8.38	3.58	5.98	24.46	9.96	17.21

Table 3: Grammatical Function Label Evaluation for Phrasal Arguments from Kübler et al. (2006)

Note that this grammatical function label evaluation is restricted to labels on phrases; grammatical function labels on words are ignored in training and testing. This results in an unbalanced comparison between Negra and TüBa-D/Z since, as discussed in section 2, TüBa-D/Z includes unary-branching phrases above all single-word arguments whereas Negra does not. In effect, single-word arguments in Negra – mainly pronouns and bare nouns – are not considered in the evaluation from Kübler et al. (2006). The result is thus a comparison of multi-word arguments in Negra to both single- and multi-word arguments in TüBa-D/Z. Recall from section 3.1 that this is not a minor difference: single-word arguments account for 38% of subjects, accusative objects, and dative objects in Negra.

As discussed in the data preparation section, Negra was modified for our experiment so as not to provide the parser with the grammatical function labels for single word phrases as part of the perfect tags provided. This evaluation handles multiple categories of arguments, not just NPs, so it focuses solely on the grammatical function labels, ignoring the phrasal categories. For example, in Negra an NP-OA in a parse is considered a correct accusative object even if the OA label in the gold standard has the category MPN. The results are shown in Table 4.

	Negra			TüBa-D/Z		
	Prec	Rec	F	Prec	Rec	F
Subj	69.69	69.12	69.42	65.74	72.24	68.99
Acc	48.17	50.97	49.57	41.37	46.81	44.09
Dat	20.93	15.22	18.08	21.40	11.51	16.46

Table 4: Grammatical Function Label Evaluation

In contrast to the results for NP grammatical functions of Kübler et al. (2006) we saw in Table 3, Negra and TüBa-D/Z perform quite similarly overall, with Negra slightly outperforming TüBa-D/Z for all types of arguments.

These results also form a clear contrast to the PARSEVAL results we saw in Table 2. Contrary to the finding in Kübler et al. (2006), the PARSEVAL evaluation does not echo the grammatical function label evaluation. In keeping with the results from Rehbein and van Genabith (2007a), we find that PARSEVAL is not an adequate predictor of performance in an evaluation targeting the functor-argument structure of the sentence for comparisons between PCFG parsers trained on corpora with different annotation schemes.

3.4.2 Labeled Dependency Triple Evaluation

While determining the grammatical function of an element is an important part of determining the functor-argument structure of a sentence, the other necessary component is determining the head of each function. To evaluate whether both the functor and the argument have been correctly found, an evaluation of labeled dependency triples is needed. As in the previous section, we focus on the grammatical function labels for arguments of verbs. To complete a labeled dependency triple for each argument, we additionally need to locate the lexical verbal head.

In Negra, the head is the sister of an argument marked with the function label "HD", however

[9]Genitive objects are also annotated in both corpora, but they are too infrequent to provide meaningful results. As discussed in Rehbein and van Genabith (2007b), labels such as subject (SB for Negra, ON for TüBa-D/Z) are not necessarily comparable in all instances, but such cases are infrequent.

heads are only marked for a subset of the phrase categories: S, VP, AP, and AVP.[10] This subset includes the phrase categories that contain verbs and their arguments, S and VP. In our experiment, the parser finds the HD grammatical function labels with a very high f-score: 99.5% precision and 96.5% recall. If the sister with the label HD is a word, then that word is the lexical head for the purposes of this dependency evaluation. If the sister with the label HD is a phrase, then a recursive search for heads within that phrase finds a lexical head. In 3.2% of cases in the gold standard, it is not possible to find a lexical head for an argument. Further methods could be applied to find the remaining heads heuristically, but we avoid the additional parameters this introduces for this evaluation by ignoring these cases.

For TüBa-D/Z, finding the head is not as simple because the verbal head and its arguments are in different topological fields. To create a parallel comparison to Negra, the finite verb from the local clause is chosen as the head for all subjects. The (finite or non-finite) main full verb is designated as the head for the accusative and dative objects. It is possible to automatically find an appropriate head verb for all but 2.7% of subjects, accusative objects, and dative objects.[11] As with Negra, only cases where a head verb can be found in the gold standard are considered in the evaluation.

As in the grammatical function evaluation in the previous section, only the grammatical function label, not the phrase category is considered in the evaluation. The results for the labeled dependency evaluation are shown in Table 5. The parser trained on Negra outperforms the one trained on TüBa-D/Z for all types of arguments.

4 Discussion of Results

Comparing PARSEVAL scores for a parser trained on the Negra and the TüBa-D/Z corpus with a grammatical function and a labeled dependency evaluation, we confirm that the PARSEVAL scores do not correlate with the scores in the other two evaluations, which given their closeness to the semantic functor argument structure make meaningful targets for evaluating parsers.

	Negra			TüBa-D/Z		
	Prec	Rec	F	Prec	Rec	F
Subj	72.84	69.03	70.93	60.52	65.98	63.25
Acc	47.96	48.80	48.38	37.39	40.83	39.11
Dat	19.56	14.01	16.79	19.32	10.39	14.85

Table 5: Labeled Dependency Evaluation

Shifting the focus to the grammatical function evaluation, we showed that a grammatical function evaluation based on phrasal arguments as provided by Kübler et al. (2006) is inadequate for comparing parsers trained on the Negra and TüBa-D/Z corpora. By introducing non-branching phrase nodes above single-word arguments in Negra, it is possible to provide a balanced comparison for the grammatical function label evaluation between Negra and TüBa-D/Z on both phrasal and single-word arguments. The models trained on both corpora perform very similarly in the grammatical function evaluation, in contrast to the claims in Kübler et al. (2006).

When the grammatical function label evaluation is extended into a labeled dependency evaluation by finding the verbal head to complete the labeled dependency triple, the parser trained on Negra outperforms that trained on TüBa-D/Z. The more significant drop in results for TüBa-D/Z compared to the grammatical function label evaluation may be due to the fact that a verbal lexical head in TüBa-D/Z is not in the same local tree as its dependents, whereas it is in Negra. The presence of intervening topological field nodes in TüBa-D/Z may make it difficult for the parser to consistently identify the elements of the dependency triple across several subtrees.

The Negra corpus annotation scheme makes it simple to identify the heads of verb arguments, but the flat NP and PP structures make it difficult to extend a labeled dependency analysis beyond verb arguments. On the other hand, TüBa-D/Z has marked heads in NPs and PPs, but it is not as easy to pair verb arguments with their heads because the verbs are in separate topological fields from their argu-

[10] However, some strings labeled as S and VP do not contain a head and thus lack a daughter with a HD function label.

[11] The relative numbers of instances where a lexical head is not found are comparable for Negra and TüBa-D/Z. Heads are not found for approximately 4% of subjects, 1% of accusative objects, and 1% of dative objects. These instances are frequently due to elision of the verb in headlines and coordinated clauses.

ments. For a constituent-based corpus annotation scheme to lend itself to a thorough labeled dependency evaluation, heads should be marked clearly for all phrase categories and all non-head elements need to have marked grammatical functions.

The presence of topological field nodes in TüBa-D/Z deserves more discussion in relation to a grammatical dependency evaluation. The corpus contains two very different types of nodes in its syntactic trees: nodes such as NP and PP that correspond to constituents and nodes such as VF (Vorfeld) and MF (Mittelfeld) that correspond to word order domains. Constituents such as NP have grammatical relations to other elements in the sentence and have identifiable heads within them, whereas nodes encoding word order domains have neither.[12] While constituents and word order domains sometimes coincide, such as the Vorfeld normally consisting of a single constituent, this is not the general case. For example, the Mittelfeld often contains multiple constituents which each stand in different grammatical relations to the verb(s) in the left and right sentence brackets (LK and VC).

Returning to the issue of finding dependencies between constituents, the intervening word order domain nodes can make it non-trivial to determine these relations in TüBa-D/Z. For example, word order domain nodes will always intervene between a verb and its arguments. In order to have all grammatical dependencies directly encoded in the treebank, it would be preferable for corpus annotation schemes to ensure that a homogeneous constituency representation can be easily obtained.

5 Future Work

An evaluation on arguments of verbs is just a first step in working towards a more complete labeled dependency evaluation. Because Negra and TüBa-D/Z do not have parallel uses of many grammatical function labels beyond arguments of verbs, a more detailed evaluation on more types of dependency relations will require a complex dependency conversion method to provide comparable results.

Since previous work on head-lexicalized parsing models for German has focused on PARSEVAL evaluations, it would also be useful to perform a labeled dependency evaluation to determine what effect head lexicalization has on particular constructions for the parsers. Because of the concerns discussed in the previous section and the difference in which types of clauses have marked heads in Negra and TüBa-D/Z, the effect of head lexicalization on the parsing results may differ for the two corpora.

6 Conclusion

Addressing the general question of how to compare parsing results for different annotation schemes, we revisited the comparison of PCFG parsing results for the Negra and TüBa-D/Z corpora. We show that these different annotation schemes lead to very significant differences in PARSEVAL scores for unlexicalized PCFG parsing models, but grammatical function label and labeled dependency evaluations for arguments of verbs show that this difference does not carry over to measures which are relevant to the semantic functor-argument structure. In contrast to Kübler et al. (2006) a grammatical function evaluation on subjects, accusative objects, and dative objects establishes that Negra and TüBa-D/Z perform similarly when all types of words and phrases appearing as arguments are taken into consideration. A labeled dependency evaluation based on grammatical relations, which links this work to current work on formalism-independent parser evaluation (e.g., Clark and Curran, 2007), shows that the parsing performance for Negra and TüBa-D/Z is comparable.

References

Adriane Boyd, 2007. Discontinuity Revisited: An Improved Conversion to Context-Free Representations. In *Proceedings of the Linguistic Annotation Workshop (LAW)*. Prague, Czech Republic.

Thorsten Brants and Oliver Plaehn, 2000. Interactive Corpus Annotation. In *Proceedings of the Second International Conference on Language Resources and Evaluation (LREC)*. Athens, Greece.

Thorsten Brants, Wojciech Skut and Hans Uszkoreit, 1999. Syntactic Annotation of a German Newspaper Corpus. In *Proceedings of the ATALA Treebank Workshop*. Paris, France.

John Carroll, Guido Minnen and Ted Briscoe, 2003. Parser evaluation: using a grammatical relation annotation scheme. In A. Abeillé (ed.), *Treebanks: Building and Using Parsed Corpora*, Kluwer, Dordrecht.

[12]While the focus in this work is on unlexicalized parsing, this also calls into question the effect of head lexicalization for a corpus that contains elements that by their nature are not the types of elements that have heads.

Stephen Clark and James Curran, 2007. Formalism-Independent Parser Evaluation with CCG and DepBank. In *Proceedings of the 45th Annual Meeting of the Association of Computational Linguistics (ACL)*. Prague, Czech Republic.

Amit Dubey, 2004. Statistical Parsing for German: Modeling Syntactic Properties and Annotation Differences. Ph.D. thesis, Universität des Saarlandes.

Amit Dubey and Frank Keller, 2003. Probabilistic Parsing Using Sister-Head Dependencies. In *Proceedings of the 41st Annual Meeting of the Association for Computational Linguistics (ACL)*. Sapporo, Japan.

Tilman Höhle, 1986. Der Begriff "Mittelfeld", Anmerkungen über die Theorie der topologischen Felder. In *Akten des Siebten Internationalen Germanistenkongresses 1985*. Göttingen, Germany.

Dan Klein and Christopher D. Manning, 2002. Fast Exact Inference with a Factored Model for Natural Language Parsing. In *Advances in Neural Information Processing Systems 15 (NIPS)*. Vancouver, British Columbia, Canada.

Sandra Kübler, 2005. How do treebank annotation schemes influence parsing results? Or how not to compare apples and oranges. In *Proceedings of the Conference on Recent Advances in Natural Language Processing (RANLP)*. Borovets, Bulgaria.

Sandra Kübler, Erhard W. Hinrichs and Wolfgang Maier, 2006. Is it really that difficult to parse German? In *Proceedings of the Conference on Empirical Methods in Natural Language Processing (EMNLP)*. Sydney, Australia.

Roger Levy and Christopher Manning, 2003. Is it harder to parse Chinese, or the Chinese Treebank? In *Proceedings of the 41st Annual Meeting of the Association for Computational Linguistics (ACL)*.

Dekang Lin, 1995. A Dependency-based Method for Evaluating Broad-Coverage Parsers. In *Proceedings of the International Joint Conference on Artificial Intelligence (IJCAI)*. Montreal, Quebec, Canada.

Ines Rehbein and Josef van Genabith, 2007a. Treebank Annotation Schemes and Parser Evaluation for German. In *Proceedings of the Joint Conference on Empirical Methods in Natural Language Processing and Computational Natural Language Learning*. Prague, Czech Republic.

Ines Rehbein and Josef van Genabith, 2007b. Why is it so difficult to compare treebanks? TIGER and TüBa-D/Z revisited. In *Proceedings of the Workshop on Treebanks and Linguistic Theories (TLT)*. Bergen, Norway.

Marga Reis, 1980. On Justifying Topological Frames: 'Positional Field' and the Order of Nonverbal Constituents in German. *Documentation et Recherche en Linguistique Allemande Contemporaine Vincennes (DRLAV)*, 22/23.

Anne Schiller, Simone Teufel and Christine Thielen, 1995. *Guidelines für das Tagging deutscher Textcorpora mit STTS*. Technical report, Universität Stuttgart, Universität Tübingen, Germany.

Helmut Schmid, 2000. *LoPar: Design and Implementation*. Arbeitspapiere des Sonderforschungsbereiches 340 No. 149, Universität Stuttgart.

Heike Telljohann, Erhard W. Hinrichs, Sandra Kübler and Heike Zinsmeister, 2005. *Stylebook for the Tübingen Treebank of Written German (TüBa-D/Z)*. Technical report, Seminar für Sprachwissenschaft, Universität Tübingen, Germany.

Parsing German with Latent Variable Grammars

Slav Petrov and Dan Klein
{petrov,klein}@cs.berkeley.edu
University of California at Berkeley
Berkeley, CA 94720

Abstract

We describe experiments on learning latent variable grammars for various German treebanks, using a language-agnostic statistical approach. In our method, a minimal initial grammar is hierarchically refined using an adaptive split-and-merge EM procedure, giving compact, accurate grammars. The learning procedure directly maximizes the likelihood of the training treebank, without the use of any language specific or linguistically constrained features. Nonetheless, the resulting grammars encode many linguistically interpretable patterns and give the best published parsing accuracies on three German treebanks.

1 Introduction

Probabilistic context-free grammars (PCFGs) underlie most high-performance parsers in one way or another (Collins, 1999; Charniak, 2000; Charniak and Johnson, 2005). However, as demonstrated in Charniak (1996) and Klein and Manning (2003), a PCFG which simply takes the empirical rules and probabilities off of a treebank does not perform well. This naive grammar is a poor one because its context-freedom assumptions are too strong in some ways (e.g. it assumes that subject and object NPs share the same distribution) and too weak in others (e.g. it assumes that long rewrites do not decompose into smaller steps). Therefore, a variety of techniques have been developed to both enrich and generalize the naive grammar, ranging from simple tree annotation and symbol splitting (Johnson, 1998; Klein and Manning, 2003) to full lexicalization and intricate smoothing (Collins, 1999; Charniak, 2000).

We view treebank parsing as the search for an optimally refined grammar consistent with a coarse training treebank. As a result, we begin with the provided evaluation symbols (such as NP, VP, etc.) but split them based on the statistical patterns in the training trees. A manual approach might take the symbol NP and subdivide it into one subsymbol NP^S for subjects and another subsymbol NP^VP for objects. However, rather than devising linguistically motivated features or splits, we take a fully automated approach, in which each symbol is split into unconstrained subsymbols. For example, NP would be split into NP-1 through NP-8. We use the Expectation-Maximization (EM) to then fit our split model to the observed trees; therein the various subsymbols will specialize in ways which may or may not correspond to our linguistic intuitions. This approach is relatively language independent, because the hidden subsymbols are induced automatically from the training trees based solely on data likelihood, though of course it is most applicable to strongly configurational languages.

In our experiments, we find that we can learn compact grammars that give the highest parsing accuracies in the 2008 Parsing German shared task. Our F1-scores of 69.8/84.0 (TIGER/TueBa-D/Z) are more than four points higher than those of the second best systems. Additionally, we investigate the patterns that are learned and show that the latent variable approach recovers linguistically interpretable phenomena. In our analysis, we pay particular attention to similarities and differences between

Proceedings of the ACL-08: HLT Workshop on Parsing German (PaGe-08), pages 33–39,
Columbus, Ohio, USA, June 2008.

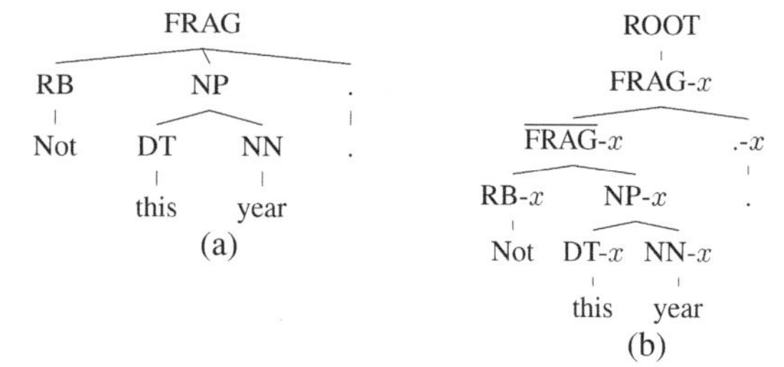

Figure 1: (a) The original tree. (b) The binarized tree with latent variables.

grammars learned from the two treebanks.

2 Latent Variable Parsing

In latent variable parsing (Matsuzaki et al., 2005; Prescher, 2005; Petrov et al., 2006), we learn rule probabilities on latent annotations that, when marginalized out, maximize the likelihood of the unannotated training trees. We use an automatic approach in which basic nonterminal symbols are alternately split and merged to maximize the likelihood of the training treebank.

In this section we briefly review the main ideas in latent variable parsing. This work has been previously published and we therefore provide only a short overview. For a more detailed exposition of the learning algorithm the reader is referred to Petrov et al. (2006). The corresponding inference procedure is described in detail in Petrov and Klein (2007). The parser, code, and trained models are available for download at `http://nlp.cs.berkeley.edu`.

2.1 Learning

Starting with a simple X-bar grammar, we use the Expectation-Maximization (EM) algorithm to learn a new grammar whose nonterminals are subsymbols of the original evaluation nonterminals. The X-bar grammar is created by binarizing the treebank trees; for each local tree rooted at an evaluation nonterminal X, we introduce a cascade of new nodes labeled $\overline{X}$ so that each node has at most two children, see Figure 1. This initialization is the absolute minimum starting grammar that distinguishes the evaluation nonterminals (and maintains separate grammars for each of them).

In Petrov et al. (2006) we show that a hierarchical split-and-merge strategy learns compact but accurate grammars, allocating subsymbols adaptively where they are most effective. Beginning with the baseline grammar, we repeatedly split and re-train the grammar. In each iteration, we initialize EM with the results of the previous round's grammar, splitting every previous symbol in two and adding a small amount of randomness (1%) to break the symmetry between the various subsymbols. Note that we split all nonterminal symbols, including the part-of-speech categories. While creating more latent annotations can increase accuracy, it can also lead to overfitting via oversplitting. Adding subsymbols divides grammar statistics into many bins, resulting in a tighter fit to the training data. At the same time, each bin has less support and therefore gives a less robust estimate of the grammar probabilities. At some point, the fit no longer generalizes, leading to overfitting.

To prevent oversplitting, we could measure the utility of splitting each latent annotation individually and then split the best ones first. However, not only is this impractical, requiring an entire training phase for each new split, but it assumes the contributions of multiple splits are independent. In fact, extra subsymbols may need to be added to several nonterminals before they can cooperate to pass information along the parse tree. This point is crucial to the success of our method: because all splits are fit simultaneously, local splits can chain together to propagate information non-locally. We therefore address oversplitting in the opposite direction; after training all splits, we measure for each one the loss in likelihood incurred by removing it. If this loss is small, the new annotation does not carry enough useful information and can be removed. Another advantage of evaluating post-hoc merges is that, unlike the likelihood gain from splitting, the likelihood loss from merging can be efficiently approximated.

To summarize, splitting provides an increasingly tight fit to the training data, while merging improves generalization and controls grammar size. In order to further overcome data fragmentation and overfitting, we also smooth our parameters along the split hierarchy. Smoothing allows us to add a larger number of annotations, each specializing in only a fraction of the data, without overfitting our training set.

2.2 Inference

At inference time, we want to use the learned grammar to efficiently and accurately compute a parse tree for a give sentence.

For efficiency, we employ a hierarchical coarse-to-fine inference scheme (Charniak et al., 1998; Charniak and Johnson, 2005; Petrov and Klein, 2007) which vastly improves inference time with no loss in test set accuracy. Our method considers the splitting history of the final grammar, projecting it onto its increasingly refined prior stages. For each such projection of the refined grammar, we estimate the projection's parameters from the source PCFG itself (rather than the original treebank), using techniques for infinite tree distributions and iterated fixpoint equations. We then rapidly pre-parse with each refinement stage in sequence, such that any item X:$[i, j]$ with sufficiently low posterior probability triggers the pruning of its further refined variants in all subsequent finer parses.

Our refined grammars G are over symbols of the form X-k where X is an evaluation symbol (such as *NP*) and k is some indicator of a subsymbol, which may encode something linguistic like a parent annotation context, but which is formally just an integer. G therefore induces a *derivation distribution* over trees labeled with split symbols. This distribution in turn induces a *parse distribution* over (projected) trees with unsplit evaluation symbols. We have several choices of how to select a tree given these posterior distributions over trees. Since computing the most likely parse tree is NP-complete (Sima'an, 1992), we settle for an approximation that allows us to (partially) sum out the latent annotation. In Petrov and Klein (2007) we relate this approximation to Goodman (1996)'s labeled brackets algorithm applied to rules and to Matsuzaki et al. (2005)'s sentence specific variational approximation. This procedure is substantially superior to simply erasing the latent annotations from the the Viterbi derivation.

2.3 Results

In Petrov and Klein (2007) we trained models for English, Chinese and German using the standard corpora and setups. We applied our latent variable model directly to each of the treebanks, without any language dependent modifications. Specifically, the same model hyperparameters (merging percentage and smoothing factor) were used in all experiments. Table 1 summarizes the results: automatically inducing latent structure is a technique that generalizes well across language boundaries and results in state of the art performance for Chinese and German. On English, the parser is outperformed by the reranked output of Charniak and Johnson (2005), but it outperforms their underlying lexicalized parser.

	$\leq$ 40 words		all	
Parser	LP	LR	LP	LR
ENGLISH				
Charniak et al. (2005)	90.1	90.1	89.5	89.6
Petrov and Klein (2007)	**90.7**	**90.5**	**90.2**	**89.9**
ENGLISH (reranked)				
Charniak et al. (2005)	**92.4**	**91.6**	**91.8**	**91.0**
GERMAN (NEGRA)				
Dubey (2005)	F_1 76.3		-	
Petrov and Klein (2007)	**80.8**	**80.7**	**80.1**	**80.1**
CHINESE				
Chiang et al. (2002)	81.1	78.8	78.0	75.2
Petrov and Klein (2007)	**86.9**	**85.7**	**84.8**	**81.9**

Table 1: Our split-and-merge latent variable approach produces the best published parsing performance on many languages.

3 Experiments

We conducted experiments on the two treebanks provided for the 2008 Parsing German shared task. Both treebanks are annotated collections of German newspaper text, covering from similar topics. They are annotated with part-of-speech (POS) tags, morphological information, phrase structure, and grammatical functions. TueBa-D/Z additionally uses topological fields to describe fundamental word order restrictions in German clauses. However, the treebanks differ significantly in their annotation schemes: while TIGER relies on crossing branches to describe long distance relationships, TueBa-D/Z uses planar tree structures with designated labels that encode long distance relationships. Additionally, the annotation in TIGER is relatively flat on the phrasal level, while TueBa-D/Z annotates more internal phrase structure.

We used the standard splits into training and de-

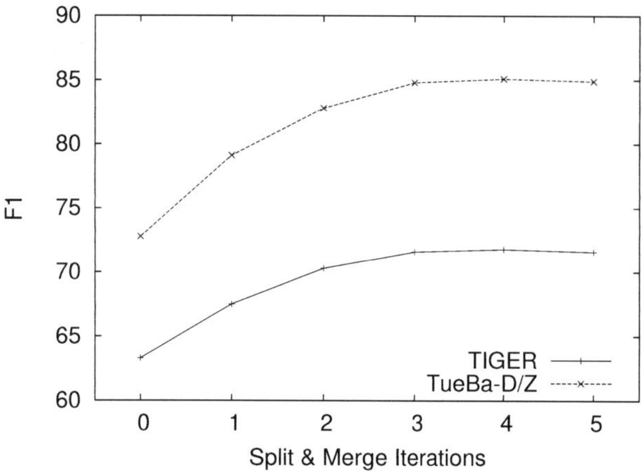

Figure 2: Parsing accuracy improves when the amount of latent annotation is increased.

velopment set, containing roughly 16,000 training trees and 1,600 development trees, respectively. All parsing figures in this section are on the development set, evaluating on constituents and grammatical functions using gold part-of-speech tags, unless noted otherwise. Note that even when we assume gold *evaluation* part-of-speech tags, we still assign probabilities to the different subsymbols of the provided evaluation tag. The parsing accuracies in the final results section are the official results of the 2008 Parsing German shared task.

3.1 Latent Annotation

As described in Section 2.1, we start with a minimal X-Bar grammar and learn increasingly refined grammars in a hierarchical split-and-merge fashion. We conjoined the constituency categories with their grammatical functions, creating initial categories like NP-PD and NP-OA which were further split automatically. Figure 2 shows how held-out accuracy improves when we add latent annotation. Our baseline grammars have low F1-scores (63.3/72.8, TIGER/TueBa-D/Z), but performance increases as the complexity of latent annotation increases. After four split-and-merge iterations, performance levels off. Interestingly, the gap in performance between the two treebanks increases from 9.5 to 13.4 F1-points. It appears that the latent variable approach is better suited for capturing the rich structure of the TueBa-D/Z treebank.

As languages vary in their phrase-internal headedness, we varied the binarization scheme, but, consistent with our experience in other languages, noticed little difference between right and left binarization. We also experimented with starting from a more constrained baseline by adding parent and sibling annotation. Adding initial structural annotation results in a higher baseline performance. However, since it fragments the grammar, adding latent annotation has a smaller effect, eventually resulting in poorer performance compared to starting from a simple X-Bar grammar. Essentially, the initial grammar is either mis- or oversplit to some degree.

	TIGER		TueBa-D/Z	
	F1	EX	F1	EX
Auto Tags	71.12	28.91	83.18	18.46
Gold Tags	71.74	34.04	85.10	20.98

Table 2: Parsing accuracies (F1-score and exact match) with gold POS tags and automatic POS tags. Many parse errors are due to incorrect tagging.

3.2 Part-of-speech tagging

When gold parts-of-speech are not assumed, many parse errors can be traced back to part-of-speech (POS) tagging errors. It is therefore interesting to investigate the influence of tagging errors on the overall parsing accuracy. For the shared task, we could assume gold POS tags: during inference we only allowed (and scored) the different subsymbols of the correct tags. However, this assumption cannot be made in a more realistic scenario, where we want to parse text from an unknown source. Table 2 compares the parsing performance with gold POS tags and with automatic tagging. While POS tagging errors have little influence on the TIGER treebank, tagging errors on TueBa-D/Z cause an substantial number of subsequent parse errors.

3.3 Two pass parsing

In the previous experiments, we conflated the phrasal categories and grammatical functions into single initial grammar symbol. An alternative is to first determine the categorical constituency structure and then to assign grammatical functions to the chosen constituents in a separate, second pass. To achieve this, we trained latent variable grammars for base constituency parsing by stripping off the grammatical functions. After four rounds of split and merge training, these grammars achieve very good constituency accuracies of 85.1/94.1 F1-score (TIGER/TueBa-D/Z). For the second pass, we estimated (but did not split) X-Bar style grammars on the grammatical functions only. Fixing the constituency structure from the first pass, we used those to add grammatical functions. Unfortunately, this approach proved to be inferior to the unified, one pass approach, giving F1-scores of only 50.0/69.4 (TIGER/TueBa-D/Z). Presumably, the degradation can be attributed to the fact that grammatical functions model long-distance relations between the constituents, which can only be captured poorly by an unsplit, highly local X-bar style grammar.

3.4 Final Results

The final results of the shared task evaluation are shown in Table 3. These results were produced by a latent variable grammar that was trained for four split-and-merge iterations, starting from an X-Bar grammar over conjoined categorical/grammatical symbols, with a left-branching binarization. Our automatic latent variable approach serves better for German disambiguation than the competing approaches, despite its being very language agnostic.

4 Analysis

In this section, we examine the learned grammars, discussing what is learned. Because the grammatical functions significantly increase the number of base categories and make the grammars more difficult to examine, we show examples from grammars that were trained for categorical constituency parsing by initially stripping off all grammatical function annotations.

4.1 Lexical Splits

Since both treebanks use the same part-of-speech categories, it is easy to compare the learned POS subcategories. To better understand what is being learned, we selected two grammars after two split and merge iterations and examined the word distributions of the subcategories of various symbols. The three most likely words for a number of POS tags are shown in Table 4. Interestingly, the subcategories learned from the different treebanks exhibit very similar patterns. For example, in both cases, the nominal category (NE) has been split into subcategories for first and last names, abbreviations and places. The cardinal numbers (CARD) have been split into subcategories for years, spelled out numbers, and other numbers. There are often subcategories distinguishing sentence initial and sentence medial placement (KOND, PDAT, ART, APPR, etc.), as well as subcategories capturing case distinctions (PDAT, ART, etc.).

A quantitative way of analyzing the complexity of what is learned is to compare the number of subcategories that our split-and-merge procedure has allocated to each category. Table 5 shows the automatically determined number of subcategories for each POS tag. While many categories have been split into comparably many of subcategories, the POS tags in the TIGER treebank have in general been refined more heavily. This increased refinement can be explained by our merging criterion. We compute the loss in likelihood that would be incurred from removing a split, and we merge back the least useful splits. In this process, lexical and phrasal splits compete with each other. In TueBa-D/Z the phrasal categories have richer internal structure and therefore get split more heavily. As a consequence, the lexical categories are often relatively less refined at any given stage than in TIGER. Having different merging thresholds for the lexical and phrasal categories would eliminate this difference and we might expect the difference in lexical refinement to become less pronounced. Of course, because of the different underlying statistics in the two treebanks, we do not expect the number of subcategories to become exactly equal in any case.

4.2 Phrasal splits

Analyzing the phrasal splits is much more difficult, as the splits can model internal as well as external context (as well as combinations thereof) and, in general, several splits must be considered jointly before their patterning can be described. Furthermore, the two treebanks use different annotation standards and different constituent categories. Overall, the phrasal categories of the TueBa-D/Z treebank have been more heavily refined, in order to better capture the rich internal structures. In both treebanks, the most heavily split categories are the noun, verb and prepositional phrase categories (NP/NX,

	TIGER			TueBa-D/Z		
	LP	LR	F1	LP	LR	F1
Berkeley Parser	**69.23**	**70.41**	**69.81**	**83.91**	**84.04**	**83.97**
Växjö Parser	67.06	63.40	65.18	76.20	74.56	75.37
Stanford Parser	58.52	57.63	58.07	79.26	79.22	79.24

Table 3: Final test set results of the 2008 Parsing German shared task (labeled precision, labeled recall and F1-score) on both treebanks (including grammatical functions and using gold part-of-speech tags).

NE (TIGER)				NE (TueBa-D/Z)			
Kohl	Klaus	SPD	Deutschland	Milosevic	Peter	K.	Berlin
Rabin	Helmut	USA	dpa	Müller	Wolfgang	W.	taz
Lafontaine	Peter	CDU	Bonn	Clinton	Klaus	de	Kosovo
CARD				**CARD**			
1996	zwei	000	zwei	1998	zwei	500	zwei
1994	drei	100	3	1999	drei	100	20
1991	vier	20	2	2000	fünf	20	18
KOND				**KOND**			
Und	und	sondern	und	Und	und	sondern	und
Doch	oder	aber	oder	Aber	oder	weder	Denn
Aber	aber	bis	sowie	Doch	aber	sowohl	oder
PDAT				**PDAT**			
Diese	dieser	diesem	-	Dieser	diese	diesem	dieser
Dieser	dieses	diese	-	Diese	dieser	dieser	diese
Dieses	diese	dieser	-	Dieses	dieses	diesen	dieses
ART				**ART**			
Die	der	der	die	Die	die	die	der
Der	des	den	der	die	Die	der	die
Das	Die	die	den	Der	das	den	den
APPR				**APPR**			
In	als	in	von	In	bis	in	von
Von	nach	von	in	Mit	Von	auf	in
Nach	vor	mit	für	Nach	Bis	mit	für
PDS				**PDS**			
Das	dessen	das	-	dem	dessen	das	Das
Dies	deren	dies	-	das	die	Das	das
Diese	die	diese	-	jene	denen	dies	diese

Table 4: The three most likely words for several part-of-speech (sub-)categories. The left column corresponds to the TIGER treebank the right column to the TueBa-D/Z treebank. Similar subcategories are learned for both treebanks.

POS	Ti	Tue	POS	Ti	Tue	POS	Ti	Tue	POS	Ti	Tue
ADJA	32	17	PIAT	8	7	VVIZU	3	2	VAIMP	1	1
NN	32	32	VAFIN	8	3	VAINF	3	3	VMPP	1	2
NE	31	32	KON	8	8	PTKNEG	3	1	PPOSS	1	1
ADV	30	15	$[	7	11	FM	3	8	PRELAT	1	1
ADJD	30	19	PROAV	7	-	PWS	2	2	NNE	1	-
VVFIN	29	5	APPRART	6	5	PWAV	2	5	APPO	1	1
VVPP	29	4	$	6	2	XY	2	2	PTKA	1	2
APPR	25	24	PDS	5	5	TRUNC	2	4	PTKANT	1	2
VVINF	18	7	PPOSAT	4	4	KOUI	2	1	PWAT	1	2
CARD	18	16	$.	4	5	PTKVZ	2	1	PRF	1	1
ART	10	7	PDAT	4	5	VAPP	2	2	PTKZU	1	1
PIS	9	14	KOUS	4	3	KOKOM	2	5	APZR	1	1
PPER	9	2	VMFIN	4	1	PROP	-	2	VMINF	1	1
PIDAT	-	9	PRELS	3	1	VVIMP	1	1	ITJ	1	2

Table 5: Automatically determined number of subcategories for the part-of-speech tags. The left column corresponds to the TIGER treebank the right column to the TueBa-D/Z treebank. Many categories are split in the same number of subcategories, but overall the TIGER categories have been more heavily refined.

PP/PX, VP/VX*) as well as the sentential categories (S/SIMPX). Categories that are rare or that have little internal structure, in contrast, have been split lightly or not at all.

5 Conclusions

We presented a series of experiments on parsing German with latent variable grammars. We showed that our latent variable approach is very well suited for parsing German, giving the best parsing figures on several different treebanks, despite being completely language independent. Additionally, we examined the learned grammars and showed examples illustrating the linguistically meaningful patterns that were learned. The parser, code, and models are available for download at `http://nlp.cs.berkeley.edu`.

References

E. Charniak and M. Johnson. 2005. Coarse-to-Fine N-Best Parsing and MaxEnt Discriminative Reranking. In *ACL'05*.

E. Charniak, S. Goldwater, and M. Johnson. 1998. Edge-based best-first chart parsing. 6th *Workshop on Very Large Corpora.*

E. Charniak. 1996. Tree-bank grammars. In *AAAI '96*, pages 1031–1036.

E. Charniak. 2000. A maximum–entropy–inspired parser. In *NAACL '00*, pages 132–139.

D. Chiang and D. Bikel. 2002. Recovering latent information in treebanks. In *COLING '02*, pages 183–189.

M. Collins. 1999. *Head-Driven Statistical Models for Natural Language Parsing*. Ph.D. thesis, UPenn.

A. Dubey. 2005. What to do when lexicalization fails: parsing German with suffix analysis and smoothing. In *ACL '05*.

J. Goodman. 1996. Parsing algorithms and metrics. *ACL '96*.

M. Johnson. 1998. PCFG models of linguistic tree representations. *Computational Linguistics*, 24:613–632.

D. Klein and C. Manning. 2003. Accurate unlexicalized parsing. In *ACL '03*, pages 423–430.

T. Matsuzaki, Y. Miyao, and J. Tsujii. 2005. Probabilistic CFG with latent annotations. In *ACL '05*.

S. Petrov and D. Klein. 2007. Improved inference for unlexicalized parsing. In *HLT-NAACL '07*.

S. Petrov, L. Barrett, R. Thibaux, and D. Klein. 2006. Learning accurate, compact, and interpretable tree annotation. In *ACL '06*.

D. Prescher. 2005. Inducing head-driven PCFGs with latent heads: Refining a tree-bank grammar for parsing. In *ECML'05*.

K. Sima'an. 1992. Computatoinal complexity of probabilistic disambiguation. *Grammars*, 5:125–151.

Parsing Three German Treebanks: Lexicalized and Unlexicalized Baselines

Anna N. Rafferty and Christopher D. Manning
Computer Science Department
Stanford University
Stanford, CA 94305
{rafferty,manning}@stanford.edu

Abstract

Previous work on German parsing has provided confusing and conflicting results concerning the difficulty of the task and whether techniques that are useful for English, such as lexicalization, are effective for German. This paper aims to provide some understanding and solid baseline numbers for the task. We examine the performance of three techniques on three treebanks (Negra, Tiger, and TüBa-D/Z): (i) Markovization, (ii) lexicalization, and (iii) state splitting. We additionally explore parsing with the inclusion of grammatical function information. Explicit grammatical functions are important to German language understanding, but they are numerous, and naïvely incorporating them into a parser which assumes a small phrasal category inventory causes large performance reductions due to increasing sparsity.

1 Introduction

Recent papers provide mixed evidence as to whether techniques that increase statistical parsing performance for English also improve German parsing performance (Dubey and Keller, 2003; Kübler et al., 2006). We provide a systematic exploration of this topic to shed light on what techniques might benefit German parsing and show general trends in the relative performance increases for each technique. While these results vary across treebanks, due to differences in annotation schemes as discussed by Kübler (2005), we also find similarities and provide explanations for the trend differences based on the annotation schemes.

We address three parsing techniques: (i) Markovization, (ii) lexicalization, and (iii) state splitting (i.e., subcategorization). These techniques are not independent, and we thus examine how lexicalization and Markovization interact, since lexicalization for German has been the most contentious area in the literature. Many of these techniques have been investigated in other work (Schiehlen, 2004; Dubey, 2004; Dubey, 2005), but, we hope that by consolidating, replicating, improving, and clarifying previous results we can contribute to the re-evaluation of German probabilistic parsing after a somewhat confusing start to initial literature in this area.

One feature of German that differs markedly from English is substantial free word order. This requires the marking of grammatical functions on phrases to indicate their syntactic function in sentences (subject, object, etc.), whereas for English these functions can be derived from configurations (Chomsky, 1965; de Marneffe et al., 2006). While some similar functions are present in English treebanks, they are used more frequently in German treebanks and many more unique functions and category-function pairings exist. Because of the relatively free word ordering in German, the usefulness of parses is substantially increased by generating them with this information. We demonstrate the difficulties introduced by naïvely concatenating these functions to categories and how this treatment interacts with the other parsing techniques. There are several avenues for improving this situation in future work. The versions of the treebanks we use here do not include case information in part-of-speech tags and we do

Proceedings of the ACL-08: HLT Workshop on Parsing German (PaGe-08), pages 40–46,
Columbus, Ohio, USA, June 2008.

Treebank	Train	Dev	≤ 40	Test	≤ 40
Tiger	20894	2611	2535	2611	2525
TüBa-D/Z	20894	2611	2611	2611	2611
Negra v2	18602	1000	975	1000	968

Table 1: Size in sentences of treebanks used in this paper. "Tiger" and "TüBa-D/Z" refer to the corpora prepared for the ACL-08 workshop shared task; the full Tiger corpus is much larger. Our Negra results are on the test set.

not use any morphological analyzer; this should be rectified in future work. A new parsing model could be written to treat separate grammatical functions for nodes as first class objects, rather than just concatenating phrasal categories and functions. Finally, assignment of grammatical functions could be left to a separate post-processing phase, which could exploit not only case information inside noun phrases but joint information across the subcategorization frames of predicates.

2 Methodology

We use the Stanford Parser (Klein and Manning, 2003b) for all experiments. An advantage of this parser for baseline experiments is that it provides clean, simple implementations of component models, with many configuration options. We show results in most instances for evaluations both with and without grammatical functions and with and without gold tags. When training and parsing with the inclusion of grammatical functions, we treat each pairing of basic category and grammatical function as one new category. Rules are learned for each such category with a separate orthographic form, with no attempt to learn general rules for nodes with the same basic category but different functions. Clearly, more sophisticated methods of handling grammatical functions exist, but our focus is on providing baseline results that are easily replicable by others.

We focus primarily on the TüBa-D/Z and Tiger corpora, training on the training sets for the ACL 2008 Workshop on Parsing German shared task and providing ablation results based on development set performance. Additionally, we show a limited number of results on the Negra corpus, using the standard training/development/test splits, defined in (Dubey and Keller, 2003). The sizes of these data sets are shown in table 1.

3 Markovization

Previous work has shown that adding vertical Markovization ((grand-)parent annotation) and using horizontal Markovization can greatly improve English parsing performance (Klein and Manning, 2003a). Several papers have already reported partially corresponding results on German: Schiehlen (2004) and Dubey (2004) reported gains of several percent for unlexicalized parsing on Negra; Kübler et al. (2006) agreed with these results for Negra, but suggests that they do not hold for TüBa-D/Z. We extend these results by examining a variety of combinations of Markovization parameters for all three corpora (TüBa-D/Z, Tiger, and Negra) in table 2. No results presented here do include grammatical functions; we present results on the interaction between these functions and Markovization in section 4.

For TüBa-D/Z, we see that adding vertical Markovization provides a substantial performance gain of about 2% (vertical Markovization = 2) for all levels of horizontal Markovization; increasing vertical Markovization improves performance only slightly further. Decreasing horizontal Markovization from the default of infinity for a standard PCFG also provides marginal gains, and decreases the number of rules learned by the parser, creating a more compact grammar. The results of Markovization on the Tiger and Negra corpora illustrate the problems of a large grammar. While a modest improvement is found by using parent annotation (vertical Markovization = 2) when horizontal Markovization is small, increasing either horizontal or vertical Markovization past this point decreases performance due to sparsity. Thus, while the general results concerning Markovization from English hold, the size of performance increase is affected appreciably by the annotation strategy.

In table 3, we show a subset of the results of various Markovization parameters when gold part-of-speech tags are used, focusing on models that performed well without gold tags and that produce relatively compact grammars. Gold tags provide 2–3% absolute improvement in F1 over tagging while parsing; slightly greater improvements are seen when the PCFG model is used individually (3–4% absolute improvement), and absolute improvement does not vary greatly between treebanks. These results are

	TüBa-D/Z			Tiger			Negra		
Horiz.	Vertical Markov Order			Vertical Markov Order			Vertical Markov Order		
Order	1	2	3	1	2	3	1	2	3
1	86.50	88.60	88.71	76.69	**77.40**	76.46	76.63	**77.20**	75.91
	(+2.76)	*(+1.21)*	*(+0.89)*	*(+3.54)*	*(+3.57)*	*(+3.27)*	*(+2.39)*	*(+2.06)*	*(+2.08)*
2	86.55	88.61	**88.84**	75.91	75.30	74.20	76.39	75.39	73.77
	(+2.63)	*(+1.22)*	*(+0.90)*	*(+3.22)*	*(+3.09)*	*(+3.10)*	*(+3.40)*	*(+2.20)*	*(+2.16)*
3	86.47	88.56	88.74	75.27	74.08	72.88	75.30	74.22	72.53
	(+2.63)	*(+1.18)*	*(+0.90)*	*(+3.36)*	*(+3.41)*	*(+2.85)*	*(+3.74)*	*(+2.12)*	*(+2.60)*
∞	86.04	88.41	88.67	74.44	73.26	71.96	74.48	73.50	71.84
	(+2.17)	*(+1.07)*	*(+0.91)*	*(+3.10)*	*(+3.02)*	*(+2.51)*	*(+3.31)*	*(+1.97)*	*(+3.02)*

Table 2: Factored parsing results for TüBa-D/Z, Tiger, and Negra when tagging is done by the parser. Numbers in italics show difference between factored parser and PCFG, where improvements over the PCFG are positive.

comparable to Maier (2006), which found 3–6% improvement using an unlexicalized PCFG; these absolute improvements hold despite the fact that the Maier (2006) parser has results with 2–4% absolute lower F1 than those in this paper.

4 Inclusion of Grammatical Functions

In this section we examine how the addition of grammatical functions for training and evaluation affects performance. As noted previously, we add grammatical functions simply by concatenating them to the dependent phrasal categories and calling each unique symbol a PCFG nonterminal; this is an obvious way to adapt an existing PCFG parser, but not a sophisticated model of grammatical functions. We also present our shared task results (table 6).

4.1 Effects on Evaluation

As shown in table 4, the inclusion of grammatical functions decreases performance by 10–15% for both treebanks. This is partially due to the increase in grammar size, creating less supporting evidence for each rule, and the fact that the parser must now discriminate amongst more categories. The larger grammar is particularly problematic for Tiger due to its flat annotation style. Adding gold tags (table 5) increases performace by 2–3%, a similar gain to that for the parsers without grammatical functions. We also see that lexicalization provides smaller gains when grammatical functions are included; we discuss this further in section 5. Finally, especially for the Tiger corpus, vertical Markovization diminishes

TüBa-D/Z	Vertical Markov Order	
Horizontal Order	1	2
1	89.66	91.69
	(+1.82)	*(+0.54)*
2	89.72	**91.71**
	(+1.56)	*(+0.43)*
∞	89.34	91.43
	(+1.39)	*(+0.29)*
Tiger	Vertical Markov Order	
Horizontal Order	1	2
1	79.39	**79.67**
	(+2.83)	*(+2.53)*
2	78.60	77.40
	(+2.74)	*(+2.22)*
∞	76.65	75.29
	(+2.50)	*(+1.94)*
Negra	Vertical Markov Order	
Horizontal Order	1	2
1	78.80	**79.51**
	(+2.39)	*(+1.55)*
2	77.92	77.43
	(+2.15)	*(+1.81)*
∞	74.44	73.26
	(+3.10)	*(+3.02)*

Table 3: Factored parsing results for TüBa-D/Z, Tiger, and Negra when gold tags are provided as input to the parser. Numbers in italics show difference between factored parser and PCFG, where improvements over the PCFG are positive.

	TueBa-D/Z		Tiger	
Horiz.	Vertical		Vertical	
Order	1	2	1	2
1	75.97	**77.21**	**60.48**	58.00
	(+2.69)	*(+1.49)*	*(+2.69)*	*(+2.24)*
2		76.96		53.68
		(+1.44)		*(+2.22)*
∞	75.24	76.66	55.36	50.94
	(+2.18)	*(+1.22)*	*(+2.50)*	*(+1.94)*

Table 4: Results for TüBa-D/Z and Tiger when grammatical functions are included and tagging is done by the parser. Numbers in italics show difference between factored parser and PCFG, where improvements over the PCFG are positive.

	TüBa-D/Z		Tiger	
Horiz.	Vertical		Vertical	
Order	1	2	1	2
1	78.91	**80.64**	**67.72**	64.93
	(+1.60)	*(+0.81)*	*(+1.16)*	*(+0.77)*
2		80.32		59.60
		(+0.69)		*(+0.67)*
∞	78.38	80.01	60.36	56.77
	(+1.33)	*(+0.59)*	*(+0.89)*	*(+0.18)*

Table 5: Results for TüBa-D/Z and Tiger when grammatical functions are included and gold tags (including grammatical functions) are given to the parser.

	TüBa-D/Z	Tiger
Petrov & Klein	**83.97**	**69.81**
Rafferty & Manning	79.24	59.44
Hall	75.37	65.18
Rafferty & Manning -gf	73.36	49.03

Table 6: Shared task results (F1) for TüBa-D/Z and Tiger when grammatical functions are included and gold tags are given to the parser. Gold tags include grammatical functions except in the case of "Rafferty & Manning -gf".

performance. Sparsity becomes too great of an issue for increased vertical annotations to be effective: the grammar grows from 11,170 rules with horizontal Markovization = 1, vertical Markovization = 1 to 39,435 rules with horizontal Markovization = ∞, vertical Markovization = 2.

TüBa-D/Z	Fact.		PCFG	
Configuration	F1	Δ	F1	Δ
$H = 1, V = 1$	87.63	+1.63	85.32	+1.58
$H = 1, V = 2$	**88.47**	−0.13	**87.31**	−0.08
$H = 2, V = 2$	88.30	−0.31	87.13	−0.26
$H = \infty, V = 1$	87.23	+1.17	85.27	+1.40
$H = \infty, V = 2$	88.18	−0.23	87.09	−0.25
Tiger	Fact.		PCFG	
Configuration	F1	Δ	F1	Δ
$H = 1, V = 1$	**72.09**	−4.60	**69.09**	−4.06
$H = 1, V = 2$	69.25	−8.15	67.24	−6.59
$H = 2, V = 2$	66.08	−9.22	64.42	−7.79
$H = \infty, V = 1$	67.58	−9.07	64.85	−6.49
$H = \infty, V = 2$	63.54	−11.75	62.21	−8.03

Table 7: Effect of adding grammatical functions information to the training data only. The difference (Δ) is from a parser with same Markovization parameters but not trained with grammatical functions.

4.2 Effects on Training Only

While training and testing with grammatical functions significantly reduces our performance, this does not necessarily mean that we cannot benefit from grammatical functions. We explored whether training with grammatical functions could improve the parser's test time performance on syntactic categories (ignoring grammatical functions), hypothesizing that the functions could provide additional information for disambiguating which rule should be applied. This test also provides evidence of whether decreased performance with grammatical functions is due to sparseness caused by the large grammar or simply that more categorization needs to be done when grammatical functions are included.

We found, as shown in table 7, that grammatical functions provide limited gains for basic categories but have no extra utility once vertical Markovization is added. These results suggest that adding grammatical functions is not only problematic due to increased categorization but because of sparseness (this task has the same categorization demands as parsing without grammatical functions considered in section 3). The Stanford Parser was initially designed under the assumption of a small phrasal category set, and makes no attempts to smooth grammar rule probabilities (smoothing only probabilities of words having a certain tag and probabilities of dependencies). While this approach is in general not optimal when many category splits are used inside the parser – smoothing helps, cf. Petrov et al. (2006) – it becomes untenable as the category set grows large, multi-faceted, and sparse. This is particularly evident given the results in table 7 that show the precipitous decline in F1 on the Tiger corpus, where the general problems are exacerbated by the flatter annotation style of Tiger.

5 Lexicalization

In the tables in section 3, we showed the utility of lexicalization for German parsing when grammatical functions are not required. This contrasts strongly with the results of (Dubey and Keller, 2003; Dubey, 2004) where no performance increases (indeed, performance decreases) are reported from lexicalization. Lexicalization shows fairly consistent 2–3% gains on the Negra and Tiger treebanks. As the number of tags increases, however, such as when grammatical functions are included, gains from lexicalization are limited due to sparseness. While useful category splits lessen the need for lexicalization, we think the diminishing gain is primarily due to problems resulting from the unsmoothed PCFG model. As the grammar becomes sparser, there are limited opportunities for the lexical dependencies to correct the output of the PCFG grammar under the factored parsing model of Klein and Manning (2003b). Indeed, as shown in table 8, the grammar becomes sufficiently sparse that for many sentences there is no tree on which the PCFG and dependency grammar can agree, and the parser falls back to simply returning the best PCFG parse. This falloff, in addition to overall issues of sparsity, helps explain the drop in performance with the addition of grammatical functions: our possible gain from lexicalized parsing is decreased by the increasing rate of failure for the factored parser. Thus, for future German work to gain from lexicalization, it may be necessary to explore smoothing the grammar or working with a diminished tagset without grammatical functions.

Lexicalized parsing focuses on identifying dependencies. As recognized by Collins (2003), identifying dependencies between words allows for better evaluation of attachment accuracy, diminishing spurious effects on labeled bracketing F1 of different annotation schemes. In particular, Rehbein and van Genabith (2007) correctly emphasize how F1 scores are very dependent on the amount of branching structure in a treebank, and are hence not validly comparable across annotation styles. We evaluate performance on identifying unlabeled dependencies between heads and modifiers, extracting dependencies automatically from the parse trees. Most heads in the TüBa-D/Z and Tiger treebanks are marked, and we use marked heads when possible for training and evaluation. When heads were not marked, we used heuristic rules to identify the likely head. Broadly consistent with the results of Rehbein and van Genabith (2007), Table 9 shows that the disparity in performance between TüBa-D/Z and Tiger is much smaller when measuring dependency accuracy rather than labeled bracketing F1, especially when using gold tags. These results also reverse the trend in our other results that adding grammatical functions greatly reduces F1. While F1 decreases or remains constant when grammatical functions are used with automatic tags, probably reflecting a decrease in accuracy on tags when using grammatical functions, they increase F1 given gold tags. These results suggest both that useful information may be gained from grammatical functions and that the dif-

	Total	Parseable	
Dataset	Sent.	w.o. GFs	with GFs
TüBa-D/Z	2611	2610	2197
Tiger	2535	2534	1592

Table 8: Number of sentences parseable by the factored lexicalized parser. If the factored model fails to return a parse, the parser returns the best PCFG parse, so the parser maintains 100% coverage.

	TüBa-D/Z	**Tiger**
Gold Tags	**91.00**	**90.21**
Auto. Tags	86.90	83.39
Gold Tags -gf	89.89	88.97
Auto. Tags -gf	86.89	85.86

Table 9: Performance (F1) on identifying dependencies in TüBa-D/Z and Tiger. Tags were either provided ("Gold Tags") or generated during parsing ("Auto. Tags"); grammatical functions were used for the first two results and omitted for the final two ("-gf").

ferences between the annotation schemes of TüBa-D/Z and Tiger may not cause as large a fundamental difference in parser performance as suggested in Kübler et al. (2006).

6 Feature Splits

Another technique shown to improve accuracy in English parsing is state splits (Klein and Manning, 2003a). We experimented with such splits in an attempt to show similar utility for German. However, despite trying a number of splits that leveraged observations of useful splits for English as well as information from grammatical functions, we were unable to find any splits that caused significant improvement for German parsing performance. Somewhat more positive results are reported by Schiehlen (2004) – in particular, his relative clause marking adds significantly to performance – although many of the other features he explores also yield little.

7 Errors by Category

In this section, we examine which categories have the most parsing errors and possible reasons for these biases. Two types of error patterns are considered: errors on particularly salient grammatical functions and overall category errors.

7.1 Grammatical Function Errors

A subset of grammatical functions was recognized by Kübler et al. (2006) as particularly important for using parsing results, so we investigated training and testing with the inclusion of these grammatical functions but without any others. These functions were the subject, dative object, and accusative object functions. We found that the three categories had distinctively different patterns of errors, although we unfortunately still do not achieve particularly high F1 for any of the individual pairings of node label and grammatical function. Note that this analysis differs from that of Kübler et al. (2006) due to our analysis of the accuracy of node labels and grammatical functions, rather than only performance on identifying these three grammatical functions (without regards to the correctness of the original node label). Overall, dative objects occur much less frequently than either of the other two types, and accusative objects occur less frequently than subjects. Consistent with sparsity causing degradations in performance, for both Tiger and TüBa-D/Z, we show the best performance on subjects, followed by accusative objects and then dative objects. For all categories, we find that these functions occur most frequently with noun phrases, and we achieve higher performance when pairing tthem with a noun phrase than with any other basic category. While Kübler et al. (2006) suggests these functions are particularly important for parsing, our low performance on dative objects (F1 between 0.00 and 0.06) may not matter a great deal given that dative objects consist of only 0.42% of development set nodes in TüBa-D/Z and 0.76% of such nodes in Tiger.

7.2 Overall Errors

One limiting factor for overall parsing accuracy is roughly defined by the number of local (one-level) trees in the test set that are present in the training set. While changes such as Markovization may allow rules to be learned that do not correspond directly to such local trees, it is unlikely that many such rules will be created. Thus, if a local tree in the test set is not represented in the training set, it is unlikely we will be able to correctly parse this sentence. The number of such local trees and the amount of test set coverage they provide varies widely between TüBa-D/Z and Tiger. Without grammatical functions, the training set for TüBa-D/Z contains 4,532 unique local trees, whereas the training set for Tiger contains 20,957; both have 20,894 complete trees. Local trees from the training set represent 79.6% of the unique local trees in the development set for TüBa-D/Z, whereas they represent 61.8% of unique local trees in Tiger's development set. This translates to 99.3% of total local trees in the development set represented in the training set for TüBa-D/Z versus 92.3% for Tiger. With grammatical functions, the number of unique local trees increases for both TüBa-D/Z and Tiger (10,464 and 32,614 trees in training, respectively), and total coverage in the development sets drop to 98.6% (TüBa-D/Z) and 87.7% (Tiger). Part of the reason for this decrease in coverage with the addition of grammatical functions, and the disparity between corpora, is a large increase in the number of possible categories for each node: from 26 to 139 categories for TüBa-D/Z and from 24 to 192 categories for Tiger.

References

Noam Chomsky. 1965. *Aspects of the Theory of Syntax.* MIT Press, Cambridge, MA.

Michael Collins. 2003. Head-driven statistical models for natural language parsing. In *Computational Linguistics*, pages 589–638.

Marie-Catherine de Marneffe, Bill MacCartney, and Christopher D. Manning. 2006. Generating typed dependency parses from phrase structure parses. In *5th International Conference on Language Resources and Evaluation (LREC 2006)*, pages 449–454.

Amit Dubey and Frank Keller. 2003. Probabilistic parsing for German using sister-head dependencies. In *ACL 41*, pages 96–103.

Amit Dubey. 2004. *Statistical Parsing for German: Modeling Syntactic Properties and Annotation Differences.* Ph.D. thesis, Universitaet des Saarlandes.

Amit Dubey. 2005. What to do when lexicalization fails: parsing German with suffix analysis and smoothing. In *ACL 43*, pages 314–21.

Dan Klein and Christopher D. Manning. 2003a. Accurate unlexicalized parsing. In *ACL 41*, pages 423–430.

Dan Klein and Christopher D. Manning. 2003b. Fast exact inference with a factored model for natural language parsing. *Advances in Neural Information Processing Systems*, 15:3–10.

Sandra Kübler, Erward W. Hinrichs, and Wolfgang Maier˙ 2006. Is it really that difficult to parse German? In *Proceedings of the 2006 Conference on Empirical Methods in Natural Language Processing.*

Sandra Kübler. 2005. How do treebank annotation schemes influence parsing results? Or how not to compare apples and oranges. In *Proceedings of RANLP 2005.*

Wolfgang Maier. 2006. Annotation schemes and their inuence on parsing results. In *Proceedings of the COLING/ACL 2006 Student Research Workshop*, pages 19–24.

Slav Petrov, Leon Barrett, Romain Thibaux, and Dan Klein. 2006. Learning accurate, compact, and interpretable tree annotation. In *ACL 44*, pages 433–440.

Ines Rehbein and Josef van Genabith. 2007. Treebank annotation schemes and parser evaluation for German. In *Proceedings of the 2007 Joint Conference on Empirical Methods in Natural Language Processing and Computational Natural Language Learning (EMNLP-CoNLL)*, pages 630–639.

Michael Schiehlen. 2004. Annotation strategies for probabilistic parsing in German. In *Proceedings of the 20th International Conference on Computational Linguistics*, pages 390–96.

A Dependency-Driven Parser for German Dependency and Constituency Representations

Johan Hall
Växjö University
Sweden
johan.hall@vxu.se

Joakim Nivre
Växjö University and
Uppsala University
Sweden
joakim.nivre@vxu.se

Abstract

We present a dependency-driven parser that parses both dependency structures and constituent structures. Constituency representations are automatically transformed into dependency representations with complex arc labels, which makes it possible to recover the constituent structure with both constituent labels and grammatical functions. We report a labeled attachment score close to 90% for dependency versions of the TIGER and TüBa-D/Z treebanks. Moreover, the parser is able to recover both constituent labels and grammatical functions with an F-Score over 75% for TüBa-D/Z and over 65% for TIGER.

1 Introduction

Is it really that difficult to parse German? Kübler et al. (2006) point out three grammatical features that could make parsing of German more difficult: finite verb placement, flexible phrase ordering and discontinuous constituents. Earlier studies by Dubey and Keller (2003) and Dubey (2005) using the Negra treebank (Skut et al., 1997) reports that lexicalization of PCFGs decrease the parsing accuracy when parsing Negra's flat constituent structures. However, Kübler et al. (2006) present a comparative study that suggests that it is not harder to parse German than for example English. By contrast, Rehbein and van Genabith (2007) study different parser evaluation metrics by simulating parser errors on two German treebanks (with different treebank annotation schemes) and they claim that the question whether German is harder to parse than English is still undecided.

This paper does not try to answer the question above, but presents a new way of parsing constituent structures that can output the whole structure with all grammatical functions. The shared task on parsing German was to parse both the constituency version and the dependency version of the two German treebanks: TIGER (Brants et al., 2002) and TüBa-D/Z (Telljohann et al., 2005). We present a dependency-driven parser that parses both dependency structures and constituent structures using an extended version of MaltParser 1.0.[1] The focus of this paper is how MaltParser parses the constituent structures with a dependency-based algorithm.

This paper is structured as follows. Section 2 briefly describes the MaltParser system, while section 3 continues with presenting the dependency parsing. Section 4 explains how a transition-based dependency-driven parser can be turned into a constituency parser. Section 5 presents the experimental evaluation and discusses the results. Finally section 6 concludes.

2 MaltParser

MaltParser is a transition-based parsing system which was one of the top performing systems on multilingual dependency parsing in the CoNLL 2006 shared task (Buchholz and Marsi, 2006; Nivre et al., 2006) and the CoNLL shared task 2007 (Nivre et al., 2007; Hall et al., 2007). The basic idea of MaltParser is to derive dependency graphs using a greedy parsing algorithm that approximates a glob-

[1] MaltParser is distributed with an open-source license and can be downloaded free of charge from following page: http://www.vxu.se/msi/users/jha/maltparser/

Proceedings of the ACL-08: HLT Workshop on Parsing German (PaGe-08), pages 47–54,
Columbus, Ohio, USA, June 2008.

ally optimal solution by making a sequence of locally optimal choices. The system is equipped with several parsing algorithms, but we have chosen to only optimize Nivre's parsing algorithm for both the dependency track and the constituency track. Nivre's algorithm is a deterministic algorithm for building labeled projective dependency structures in linear time (Nivre, 2006). There are two essential parameters that can be varied for this algorithm. The first is the arc order and we selected the arc-eager order that attaches the right dependents to their head as soon as possible. The second is the stack initialization and we chose to use an empty stack initialization that attaches root dependents with a default root label after completing the left-to-right pass over the input.

The algorithm uses two data structures: a stack to store partially processed tokens and a queue of remaining input tokens. The arc-eager transition-system has four parser actions:

1. LEFT-ARC(r): Adds an arc labeled r from the next input token to the top token of the stack, the top token is popped from the stack because it must be complete with respect to left and right dependents at this point.

2. RIGHT-ARC(r): Adds an arc labeled r from the top token of the stack to the next input token and pushes the next input token onto the stack (because it may have dependents further to the right).

3. REDUCE: Pops the top token of the stack. This transition can be performed only if the top token has been assigned a head and is needed for popping a node that was pushed in a RIGHT-ARC(r) transition and which has since found all its right dependents.

4. SHIFT: Pushes the next input token onto the stack. This is correct when the next input token has its head to the right or should be attached to the root.

MaltParser uses history-based feature models for predicting the next parser action at nondeterministic choice points. Previously, MaltParser combined the prediction of the transition with the prediction of the arc label r into one complex prediction with one feature model. The experiments presented in this paper use another prediction strategy, which divide the prediction of the parser action into several predictions. First the transition is predicted; if the transition is SHIFT or REDUCE the nondeterminism is resolved, but if the predicted transition is RIGHT-ARC or LEFT-ARC the parser continues to predict the arc label r. This prediction strategy enables the system to have three different feature models: one for predicting the transition and two for predicting the arc label r (RIGHT-ARC and LEFT-ARC). We will see in section 4 that this change makes it more feasible to encode the inverse mapping into complex arc labels for an arbitrary constituent structure without losing any information.

All symbolic features were converted to numerical features and we use the quadratic kernel $K(x_i, x_j) = (\gamma x_i^T x_j + r)^2$ of the LIBSVM package (Chang and Lin, 2001) for mapping histories to parser actions and arc labels. All results are based on the following settings of LIBSVM: $\gamma = 0.2$ and $r = 0$ for the kernel parameters, $C = 0.5$ for the penalty parameter, and $\epsilon = 1.0$ for the termination criterion. We also split the training instances into smaller sets according to the fine-grained part-of-speech of the next input token to train separate one-versus-one multi-class LIBSVM-classifiers.

3 Dependency Parsing

Parsing sentences with dependency structures like the one in Figure 1 is straightforward using MaltParser. During training, the parser reconstructs the correct transition sequence needed to derive the gold standard dependency graph of a sentence. This involves choosing a label r for each arc, which in a pure dependency structure is an atomic symbol. For example, in Figure 1, the arc from *hat* to *Beckmeyer* is labeled SUBJ. This is handled by training a separate labeling model for RIGHT-ARC and LEFT-ARC. During parsing, the sentence is processed in the same way as during training except that the parser requests the next transition from the transition classifier. If the predicted transition is an arc transition (RIGHT-ARC or LEFT-ARC), it then asks the corresponding classifier for the arc label r.

One complication when parsing the dependency version of the two German treebanks is that they

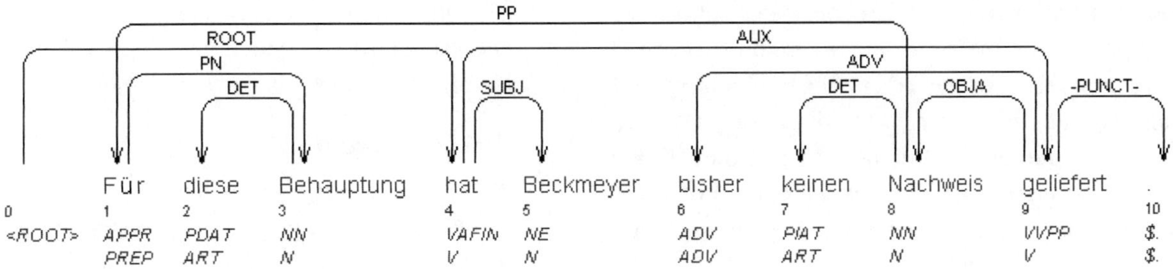

Figure 1: The sentence "For this statement has Beckmeyer until now not presented any evidence." is taken from dependency version of TüBa-D/Z treebank.

contain non-projective structures, such as the dependency graph illustrated in Figure 1. Nivre's parsing algorithm only produces projective dependency structures, and therefore we used pseudo-projective parsing for recovering non-projective structures. The training data are projectivized and information about these transformations is encoded into the arc labels to enable deprojectivizition of the parser output (Nivre and Nilsson, 2005).

4 Constituency Parsing

This section explains how a transition-based dependency parser can be used for parsing constituent structures. The basic idea is to use the common practice of transforming a constituent structure into a dependency graph and encode the inverse mapping with complex arc labels. Note that the goal is not to create the best dependency representation of a constituent structure. Instead the main objective is to find a general method to transform constituency to dependency so that is easy to do the inverse transformation without losing any information. Moreover, another goal is to transform the constituent structures so that it is feasible for a transition-based dependency parser to induce a parser model based on the resulting dependency graphs and during parsing use this parser model to derive constituent structures with the highest accuracy possible. Hence, the transformation described below is not designed with the purpose of deriving a linguistically sound dependency graph from a constituent structure.

Our strategy for turning a dependency parser into a constituency parser can be summarized with the following steps:

1. Identify the lexical head of every constituent in the constituent structure.
2. Identify the head of every token in the dependency structure.
3. Build a labeled dependency graph that encodes the inverse mapping in the arc labels.
4. Induce a parser model based on the labeled dependency graphs.
5. Use the induced parser model to parse new sentences into dependency graphs.
6. Derive the constituent structure by performing the inverse mapping encoded in the dependency graph produced in step 5.

4.1 Identify the Heads

The first steps are basically the steps that are used to convert a constituent structure to a dependency structure. One way of doing this is to traverse the constituent structure from the root node and identify the head-child and the lexical head of all constituent nodes in a recursive depth-first search. Usually this process is governed by pre-defined head-finding rules that define the direction of the search for each distinct constituent label. Moreover, it is quite common that the head-finding rules define some kind of priority lists over which part of speech or grammatical function is the more preferable head-child.

For our experiment on German we have kept this search of the head-child and lexical head very simple. For the TIGER treebank we perform a left-to-right search to find the leftmost lexical child. If no lexical child can be found, the head-child of the constituent will be the leftmost constituent child and the lexical head will be the lexical child of the head child recursively. For the TüBa-D/Z treebank we got higher accuracy if we varied the direction of search according to the label of the target constituent.[2] We also tried more complex and linguistically motivated head rules, but unfortunately no improvement in accuracy could be found. We want to stress that the use of more complex head rules was done late in the parser optimization process and it would not be a surprise if more careful experiments resulted in the opposite conclusion.

Given that all constituents have been assigned a lexical head it is a straightforward process to identify the head and the dependents of all input tokens. The algorithm investigates, for each input token, the containing constituent's lexical head, and if the token is not the lexical head of the constituent it takes the lexical head as its head in the dependency graph; otherwise the head will be assigned the lexical head of a higher constituent in the structure. The root of the dependency graph will be the lexical head of the root of the constituent structure.

4.2 Build a Labeled Dependency Graph

The next step builds a labeled dependency representation that encodes the inverse mapping in the arc labels of the dependency graph. Each arc label is a quadruple consisting of four sublabels (*dependency relation*, *head relations*, *constituent labels*, *attachment*). The meaning of each sublabel is following:

- The *dependency relation* is the grammatical function of the highest constituent of which the dependent is the lexical head.
- The *head relations* encode the path of function labels from the dependent to the highest constituent of which is the lexical head (with path elements separated by |).
- The *constituent labels* encode the path of constituent labels from the dependent to the highest constituent of which is the lexical head (with path elements separated by |).
- The *attachment* is a non-negative integer i that encodes the attachment level of the highest constituent of which it is the lexical head.

4.3 Encoding Example

Figure 2 illustrates the procedure of encoding the constituency representation as a dependency graph with complex arc labels for a German sentence. The constituent structure is shown above the sentence and below we can see the resulting dependency graph after the transformation. We want to stress that the resulting dependency graph is not linguistically sound, and the main purpose is to demonstrate how a constituent structure can be encoded in a dependency graph that have all information need for the inverse transformation.

For example, the constituent MF has no lexical child and therefore the head-child is the leftmost constituent NX. The lexical head of MF is the token *Beckmeyer* because it is the lexical head of NX. For the same reason the lexical head of the constituent SIMPX is the token *Für* and this token will be the head of the token *Beckmeyer*, because SIMPX dominates MF. In the dependency graph this is illustrated with an arc from the head *Für* to its dependent *Beckmeyer*.

The arc *Für* to *Beckmeyer* is labeled with a complex label (??, HD|ON, NX|MF, 2), which consists of four sublabels. The first sublabel is the grammatical function above MF and because this is missing a dummy label ?? is used instead. The sublabel HD|ON encodes a sequence of head relations from the lexical head *Beckmeyer* to MF. The constituent labels are encoded in the same way in the third sublabel NX|MF. Finally, the fourth sublabel indicates the attachment level of the constituent MF. In this case, MF should be attached to the constituent two levels up in the structure with respect to the head *Für*.[3]

The two arcs *diese* to *Behauptung* and *keinen* to *Nachweis* both have the complex arc label (HD, *, *, 0), because the tokens *Behauptung* and *Nachweis* are attached to a constituent without being a lexical head of any dominating constituent. Consequently, there are no sequences of head relations and constituent

[2]It was beneficial to make a right-to-left search for the following labels: ADJX, ADVX, DM, DP, NX, PX

[3]If the fourth sublabel had an attachment level of 1, then the constituent MF would be attached to the constituent VF instead of the constituent SIMPX.

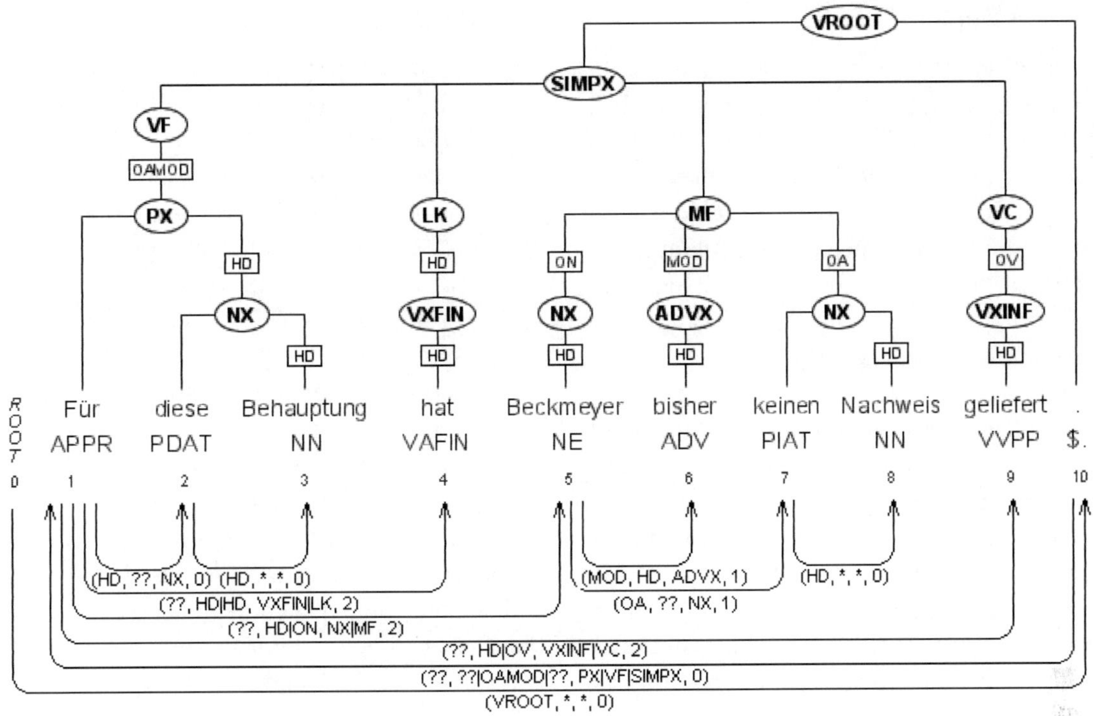

Figure 2: The sentence "For this statement has Beckmeyer until now not presented any evidence." is taken from TüBa-D/Z treebank and show the encoding of a constituent structure as a dependency graph.

labels to encode, and these are therefore marked *. The encoding of the virtual root VROOT is treated in a special way and the label VROOT is regarded as a dependency relation instead of a constituent label.

If we compare the dependency graphs in Figure 1 and Figure 2, we can see large differences. The more linguistically motivated dependency graph (LDG) in Figure 1 has a completely difference structure and different arc labels compared to the automatically generated dependency graph (ADG) in Figure 2. There are several reasons, some of which are listed here:

- Different conversions strategies: LDG is based on a conversion that sometimes leads to non-projective structures for non-local dependencies. For example, in Figure 2, the extracted PP *Für diese Behauptung* has the grammatical function OAMOD, which indicates that it is a modifier (MOD) of a direct object (OA) elsewhere in the structure (in this case *keinen Nachweis*). In LDG, this is converted to a non-projective dependency from *Nachweis* to *Für* (with the label PP). No such transformtion is attempted in ADC, which simply attaches *Für* to the lexical head of the containing constituent.

- Different head-finding rules: ADG are derived without almost no rules at all. Most likely, the conversion of LDG makes use of several linguistically sound head-finding rules. A striking difference is the root of the dependency graph, where LDG has its root at the linguistically motivated token *hat*. Whereas ADG has its root at the end of the sentence, because the leftmost lexical child of the virtual root VROOT is the punctuation.

- Different arc labels: ADG encodes the constituent structure in the complex arc labels to be able to recover the constituent structure, whereas LDG have linguistically motivated dependency relations that are not present in the constituent structure.

We believe that our simplistic approach can be further improved by using ideas from the conversion process of LDG.

4.4 Inverse Mapping

The last step of our presented strategy is to make the inverse transformation from a dependency graph to a constituent structure. This is done by a bottom-up and top-down process of the dependency graph. First we iterate over all tokens in the dependency graph and restore the sequence of constituent nodes with constituent labels and grammatical functions for each individual token using the information of the sublabels *head relations* and *constituent labels*. After this bottom-up process we have the lineage of constituents for each token where the token is the lexical head. The top-down process then traverse the dependency graph recursively from the root with pre-order depth-first search. For each token, the highest constituent of the lineage of the token is attached to its head lineage at an attachment level according to the sublabel *attachment*. Finally, the edge between the dominating constituent and the highest constituent of the lineage is labeled with a grammatical function according to the sublabel *dependency relation*.

4.5 Parsing

For the constituency versions of both TIGER and TüBa-D/Z we can recover the constituent structure without any loss of information, if we transform from constituency to dependency and back again to constituency. During parsing we predict the sublabels separately with separate feature models for RIGHT-ARC and LEFT-ARC. Moreover, the parsed constituent structure can contain discontinuous constituency because of wrong attachment levels of constituents. To overcome this problem, the structure is post-processed and the discontinuous constituents are forced down in the structure so that the parser output can be represented in a nested bracketing format.

5 Experiments

The shared task on parsing German consisted of parsing either the dependency version or the constituency version of two German treebanks, although we chose to parse both versions. This section first presents the data sets used. We continue with a brief overview of how we optimized the four different parser models. Finally, the results are discussed.

5.1 Data Sets

The prepared training and development data distributed by the organizers were based on the German TIGER (Brants et al., 2002) and TüBa-D/Z (Telljohann et al., 2005) treebanks, one dependency and one constituency version for each treebank. Both treebanks contain German newspaper text and the prepared data sets were of the same size. The development set contained 2611 sentences and the training set contained 20894 sentences. The dependency and constituency versions contained the same set of sentences.

The dependency data were formated according to the CoNLL dependency data format.[4] The LEMMA, FEATS, PHEAD and PDEPREL columns of the CoNLL format were not used at all.

The constituency data have been converted into a bracketing format similar to the Penn Treebank format. All trees are dominated by a VROOT node and all constituents are continuous. The test data consisted of sentences with gold-standard part-of-speech tags and also the gold-standard grammatical functions attached to the part-of-speech tags. Unfortunately, we were not aware of that the grammatical functions attached to the part-of-speech tags should be regarded as input to the parser and therefore our presented results are based on not using the grammatical functions attached to the part-of-speech tags as input to the parser.

We divided the development data into two sets, one set used for parser optimization (80%) and the other 20% we saved for final preparation before the release of the test data. For the final test run we trained parser models on all the data, both the training data and the development data.

5.2 Parser optimization

We ran several experiments to optimize the four different parser models. The optimization of the dependency versions was conducted in a way similar to the parser optimization of MaltParser in the CoNLL shared tasks (Nivre et al., 2006; Hall et al., 2007). A new parameter for the extended version

[4]More information about the CoNLL dependency data format can be found at: http://nextens.uvt.nl/ conll/#dataformat. Yannick Versley has done work of converting both treebanks to a dependency annotation that is similar to the Hamburg dependency format.

of MaltParser 1.0 is the prediction strategy, where we could choose between combining the prediction of the transition with the prediction of the arc label into one complex prediction or dividing the prediction of the parser action into two predictions (one model for predicting the transition and two models for predicting the arc label depending on the outcome of the transition-model). It was beneficial to use the divided predication strategy for all four data sets. In the next step we performed a feature optimization with both forward and backward selection, starting from a model extrapolated from many previous experiments on different languages. Because we chose to use the divided predication strategy this step was more complicated compared to using the combined strategy, because we needed to optimize three feature models (one transition-model and two arc-label models, one for RIGHT-ARC and one for LEFT-ARC).

The optimization of the constituency versions was even more complex because each parser model contained nine feature models (one transition-model, two models for each sublabel). Another problem for the parser optimization was the fact that we tried out new ideas and for example changed the encoding a couple of times. Due to the time constraints of the shared task it was not possible to start parser optimization all over again for every change. We also performed some late experiments with different head-finding rules to make the intermediate dependency graphs more linguistically sound, but unfortunately these experiments did not improve the parsing accuracy. We want to emphasize that the time for developing the extended version of MaltParser to handle constituency was severely limited, especially the implementation of head-finding rules, so it is very likely that head-finding rules can improve parsing accuracy after more careful testing and experiments.

5.3 Results and Discussion

The results based on the prepared test data for the dependency and constituency tracks are shown in table 1. The label attachment score (LAS) was used by the organizer for evaluating the dependency versions, that is, the proportion of tokens that are assigned the correct head and the correct arc label (punctuation included). We can see that the dependency results are close to 90% for both the treebanks, 90.80 for TIGER and 88.64 for Tüba-D/Z, which were the unchallenged best scores in the shared task. The highest score on parsing German in the CoNLL-X shared task was obtained by the system of McDonald et al. (2006) with a LAS of 87.34 based on the TIGER treebank, but we want to stress that these results are not comparable due to different data sets (and a different policy regarding the inclusion of punctuation).

	Dependency	**Constituency**		
Treebank	**LAS**	**LP**	**LR**	**LF**
TIGER	90.80	67.06	63.40	65.18
TüBa-D/Z	88.64	76.44	74.79	75.60

Table 1: The results for the extended version of MaltParser 1.0 in the shared task on parsing German dependency and constituency representations.

The constituency versions were evaluated according to the labeled recall (LR), labeled precision (LP) and labeled F-score (LF). Labeled in this context means that both the constituent label and the grammatical function should agree with the gold-standard, but grammatical functions labeling the edge between a constituent and a token were not included in the evaluation. The labeled F-scores are 75.60 for Tüba-D/Z and 65.18 for TIGER and these results are the second best results in the shared task out of three systems. We want to emphasize that the results may not be strictly comparable because of different use of the grammatical functions attached to the parts of speech in the bracketing format. We did not use these grammatical functions as input, instead these were assigned by the parser. Our results are competitive if we compare with Kübler et al. (2006), who report 51.41 labeled F-score on the Negra treebank and 75.33 on the TüBa-D/Z treebank using the unlexicalized, markovized PCFG version of the Stanford parser.

We believe that our results for the constituency representations can be improved upon by investigating different methods for encoding the inverse mapping in the complex arc labels and performing a more careful evaluation of head-finding rules to derive a more linguistically sound dependency representation. Another interesting line of future work is to try to parse discontinuous constituents by using a non-projective parsing algorithm like the Covington algorithm (Covington, 2001) or using pseudo-projective parsing for discontinuous constituency parsing (Nivre and Nilsson, 2005).

6 Conclusion

We have shown that a transition-based dependency-driven parser can be used for parsing German with both dependency and constituent representations. We can report state-of-the-art results for parsing the dependency versions of two German treebanks, and we have demonstrated, with promising results, how a dependency parser can parse full constituent structures by encoding the inverse mapping in complex arc labels of the dependency graph. We believe that this method can be improved by using, for example, head-finding rules.

Acknowledgments

We want to thank the treebank providers for making the data available for the shared task and the organizers for their efforts in organizing it. Thanks also to two reviewers for useful comments.

References

Sabine Brants, Stefanie Dipper, Silvia Hansen, Wolfgang Lezius, and George Smith. 2002. The TIGER Treebank. In *Proceedings of the Workshop on Treebanks and Linguistic Theories Sozopol*, pages 1–18.

Sabine Buchholz and Erwin Marsi. 2006. CoNLL-X Shared Task on Multilingual Dependency Parsing. In *Proceedings of the Tenth Conference on Computational Natural Language Learning (CoNLL-X)*, pages 149–164.

Chih-Chung Chang and Chih-Jen Lin. 2001. LIBSVM: A Library for Support Vector Machines.

Michael A. Covington. 2001. A Fundamental Algorithm for Dependency Parsing. In *Proceedings of the 39th Annual ACM Southeast Conference*, pages 95–102.

Amit Dubey and Frank Keller. 2003. Probabilistic Parsing for German using Sister-Head Dependencies. In *Proceedings of the 41st Annual Meeting of the Association for Computational Linguistics (ACL)*, pages 96–103.

Amit Dubey. 2005. What to do when Lexicalization fails: Parsing German with Suffix Analysis and Smoothing. In *Proceedings of the 43rd Annual Meeting of the Association for Computational Linguistics (ACL)*, pages 314–321.

Johan Hall, Jens Nilsson, Joakim Nivre, Gülşen Eryiğit, Beáta Megyesi, Mattias Nilsson, and Markus Saers. 2007. Single Malt or Blended? A Study in Multilingual Parser Optimization. In *Proceedings of the CoNLL Shared Task Session of EMNLP-CoNLL 2007*, pages 933–939.

Sandra Kübler, Erhard W. Hinrichs, and Wolfgang Maier. 2006. Is it Really that Difficult to Parse German. In *Proceedings of the 2006 Conference on Empirical Methods in Natural Language Processing (EMNLP 2006)*, pages 111–119.

Ryan McDonald, Kevin Lerman, and Fernando Pereira. 2006. Multilingual Dependency Analysis with a Two-Stage Discriminative Parser. In *Proceedings of the Tenth Conference on Computational Natural Language Learning (CoNLL-X)*, pages 216–220.

Joakim Nivre and Jens Nilsson. 2005. Pseudo-Projective Dependency Parsing. In *Proceedings of the 43rd Annual Meeting of the Association for Computational Linguistics (ACL)*, pages 99–106.

Joakim Nivre, Johan Hall, Jens Nilsson, Gülşen Eryiğit, and Svetoslav Marinov. 2006. Labeled Pseudo-Projective Dependency Parsing with Support Vector Machines. In *Proceedings of the Tenth Conference on Computational Natural Language Learning (CoNLL-X)*, pages 221–225.

Joakim Nivre, Johan Hall, Sandra Kübler, Ryan McDonald, Jens Nilsson, Sebastian Riedel, and Deniz Yuret. 2007. The CoNLL 2007 Shared Task on Dependency Parsing. In *Proceedings of the CoNLL Shared Task Session of EMNLP-CoNLL 2007*, pages 915–932.

Joakim Nivre. 2006. *Inductive Dependency Parsing*. Springer.

Ines Rehbein and Josef van Genabith. 2007. Treebank Annotation Schemes and Parser Evaluation for German. In *Proceedings of the 2007 Joint Conference on Empirical Methods in Natural Language Processing and Computational Natural Language Learning (EMNLP-CoNLL 2007)*, pages 630–639.

Wojciech Skut, Brigitte Krenn, Thorsten Brants, and Hans Uszkoreit. 1997. An Annotation Scheme for Free Word Order Languages. In *Proceedings of the Fifth Conference on Applied Natural Language Processing (ANLP)*, pages 314–321.

Heike Telljohann, Erhard W. Hinrichs, Sandra Kübler, and Heike Zinsmeister. 2005. Stylebook for the Tübingen Treebank of Written German (TüBa-D/Z). Seminar für Sprachwissenschaft, Universität Tübingen, Germany.

The PaGe 2008 Shared Task on Parsing German*

Sandra Kübler
Department of Linguistics
Indiana University
Bloomington, IN, USA
skuebler@indiana.edu

Abstract

The ACL 2008 Workshop on Parsing German features a shared task on parsing German. The goal of the shared task was to find reasons for the radically different behavior of parsers on the different treebanks and between constituent and dependency representations. In this paper, we describe the task and the data sets. In addition, we provide an overview of the test results and a first analysis.

1 Introduction

German is one of the very few languages for which more than one syntactically annotated resource exists. Other languages for which this is the case include English (with the Penn treebank (Marcus et al., 1993), the Susanne Corpus (Sampson, 1993), and the British section of the ICE Corpus (Wallis and Nelson, 2006)) and Italian (with ISST (Montegmagni et al., 2000) and TUT (Bosco et al., 2000)). The three German treebanks are Negra (Skut et al., 1998), TIGER (Brants et al., 2002), and TüBa-D/Z (Hinrichs et al., 2004). We will concentrate on TIGER and TüBa-D/Z here; Negra is annotated with an annotation scheme very similar to TIGER but is smaller. In contrast to other languages, these two treebanks are similar on many levels: Both treebanks are based on newspaper text, both use the STTS part of speech (POS) tagset (Thielen and Schiller, 1994), and both use an annotation scheme based on constituent structure augmented with grammatical functions. However, they differ in the choices made in the annotation schemes, which makes them ideally suited for an investigation of how these decisions influence parsing accuracy in different parsers.

On a different level, German is an interesting language for parsing because of the syntactic phenomena in which the language differs from English, the undoubtedly most studied language in parsing: German is often listed as a non-configurational language. However, while the word order is freer than in English, the language exhibits a less flexible word order than more typical non-configurational languages. A short overview of German word order phenomena is given in section 2.

The structure of this paper is as follows: Section 2 discusses three characteristics of German word order, section 3 provides a definition of the shared task, and section 4 gives a short overview of the treebanks and their annotation schemes that were used in the shared task. In section 5, we give an overview of the participating systems and their results.

2 German Word Order

In German, the order of non-verbal phrases is relatively free, but the placement of the verbal elements is determined by the clause type. Thus, we will first describe the placement of the finite verb, then we will explain phrasal ordering, and finally we will look at discontinuous constituents.

*I am very grateful to Gerald Penn, who suggested this workshop and the shared task, took over the biggest part of the workshop organization and helped with the shared task.

Proceedings of the ACL-08: HLT Workshop on Parsing German (PaGe-08), pages 55–63,
Columbus, Ohio, USA, June 2008.

2.1 Verb Placement

In German, the clause type determines the placement of finite verbs: In non-embedded declarative clauses, as in (1a), the finite verb is in second position (V2). In yes/no questions, as in (1b), the finite verb is the clause-initial constituent (V1), and in embedded clauses, as in (1c), it appears clause finally (Vn).

(1) a. Der Mann hat das Auto gekauft.
The man has the car bought

'The man has bought the car.'

b. Hat der Mann das Auto gekauft?
Has the man the car bought

'Has the man bought the car?'

a. dass der Mann das Auto gekauft hat.
that the man the car bought has

'... that the man has bought the car.'

All non-finite verbs appear at the right periphery of the clause (cf. 2), independently of the clause type.

(2) Der Mann sollte das Auto gekauft haben.
The man should the car bought have

'The man should have bought the car.'

2.2 Flexible Phrase Ordering

Apart from the fixed placement of the verbs, the order of the non-verbal elements is flexible. In (3), any of the four complements and adjuncts of the main verb *(ge)geben* can be in sentence-initial position, depending on the information structure of the sentence.

(3) a. Das Kind hat dem Mann gestern den
The child has the man yesterday the
Ball gegeben.
ball given

'The child has given the ball to the man yesterday.'

b. Dem Mann hat das Kind gestern den Ball gegeben.

c. Gestern hat das Kind dem Mann den Ball gegeben.

d. Den Ball hat das Kind gestern dem Mann gegeben.

In addition, the ordering of the elements that occur between the finite and the non-finite verb forms is also free so that there are six possible linearizations for each of the examples in (3a-d).

One exception to the free ordering of non-verbal elements is the ordering of pronouns. If the pronouns appear to the right of the finite verb in V1 and V2 clauses, they are adjacent to the finite verb in fixed order.

(4) Gestern hat sie sie ihm gegeben.
Yesterday has she her/them him given.

'Yesterday, she gave her/them to him.'

In (4), three pronouns are present. Although the pronoun *sie* is ambiguous between nominative/accusative singular and nominative/accusative plural, the given example is unambiguous with respect to case since the nominative precedes the accusative, which in turn precedes the dative.

Due to the flexible phrase ordering, the grammatical functions of constituents in German, unlike in English, cannot be deduced from the constituents' location in the constituent tree. As a consequence, parsing approaches to German need to be based on treebank data which contain a combination of constituent structure and grammatical functions – for parsing and evaluation. For English, in contrast, grammatical functions are often used internally in parsers but suppressed in the final parser output.

2.3 Discontinuous Constituents

Another characteristic of German word order is the frequency of discontinuous constituents. The sentence in (5) shows an extraposed relative clause that is separated from its head noun *das Buch* by the non-finite verb *gelesen.*

(5) Der Mann hat das Buch gelesen, das ich
The man has the book read, which I
ihm empfohlen habe.
him recommended have

'The man read the book that I recommended to him.'

In German, it is also possible to partially front VPs, such as in sentence (6). This sentence is taken from the TüBa-D/Z treebank.

(6) Für den Berliner Job qualifiziert hat sich
For the Berlin job qualified has himself
Zimmermann auch durch seinen Blick fürs
Zimmermann also by his view for the
finanziell Machbare.
financially doable

'Zimmermann qualified for the job in Berlin partially because of his view for what is financially feasible.'

Here, the canonical word order would be *Zimmermann hat sich auch durch seinen Blick fürs finanziell Machbare für den Berliner Job qualifiziert.*

Such discontinuous structures occur frequently in the TIGER and TüBa-D/Z treebanks and are handled differently in the two annotation schemes, as will be discussed in more detail in section 4.

3 Task Definition

In this section, we give the definition of the shared task. We provided two subtasks: parsing constituent structure and parsing the dependency representations. Both subtasks involved training and testing on data from the two treebanks, TIGER and TüBa-D/Z. The dependency format was derived from the constituent format so that the sentences were identical in the two versions. The participants were given training sets, development sets, and test sets of the two treebanks. The training sets contained 20894 sentences per treebank, the development and test set consisted of 2611 sentences each. The test sets contained gold standard POS labels. In these sets, sentence length was restricted to a maximum of 40 words. Since for some sentences in both treebanks, the annotation consists of more than one tree, all trees were joined under a virtual root node, *VROOT*.

Since some parsers cannot assign grammatical functions to part of speech tags, these grammatical functions were provided for the test data as attached to the POS tags. Participants were asked to perform a test without these functions if their parser was equipped to provide them. Two participants did submit these results, and in both cases, these results were considerably lower.

Evaluation for the constituent version consisted of the PARSEVAL measures precision, recall, and F_1 measure. All these measures were calculated on combinations of constituent labels and grammatical functions. Part of speech labels were not considered in the evaluation. Evaluation for the dependency version consisted of labeled and unlabeled attachment scores. For this evaluation, we used the scripts provided by the CoNLL shared task 2007 on dependency parsing (Nivre et al., 2007).

4 The Treebanks

The two treebanks used for the shared task were the TIGER Corpus, (Brants et al., 2002) version 2, and the TüBa-D/Z treebank (Hinrichs et al., 2004; Telljohann et al., 2006), version 3. Both treebanks use German newspapers as their data source: the Frankfurter Rundschau newspaper for TIGER and the 'die tageszeitung' (taz) newspaper for TüBa-D/Z. The average sentence length is very similar: In TIGER, sentences have an average length of 17.0, and in TüBa-D/Z, 17.3. This can be regarded as an indication that the complexity of the two texts is comparable. Both treebanks use the same POS tagset, STTS (Thielen and Schiller, 1994), and annotations based on phrase structure grammar, enhanced by a level of predicate-argument structure.

4.1 The Constituent Data

Despite all the similarities presented above, the constituent annotations differ in four important aspects: 1) TIGER does not allow for unary branching whereas TüBa-D/Z does; 2) in TIGER, phrase internal annotation is flat whereas TüBa-D/Z uses phrase internal structure; 3) TIGER uses crossing branches to represent long-distance relationships whereas TüBa-D/Z uses a pure tree structure combined with functional labels to encode this information. The two treebanks also use different notions of grammatical functions: TüBa-D/Z defines 36 grammatical functions covering head and non-head information, as well as subcategorization for complements and modifiers. TIGER utilizes 51 grammatical functions. Apart from commonly accepted grammatical functions, such as *SB* (subject) or *OA* (accusative object), TIGER grammatical functions in-

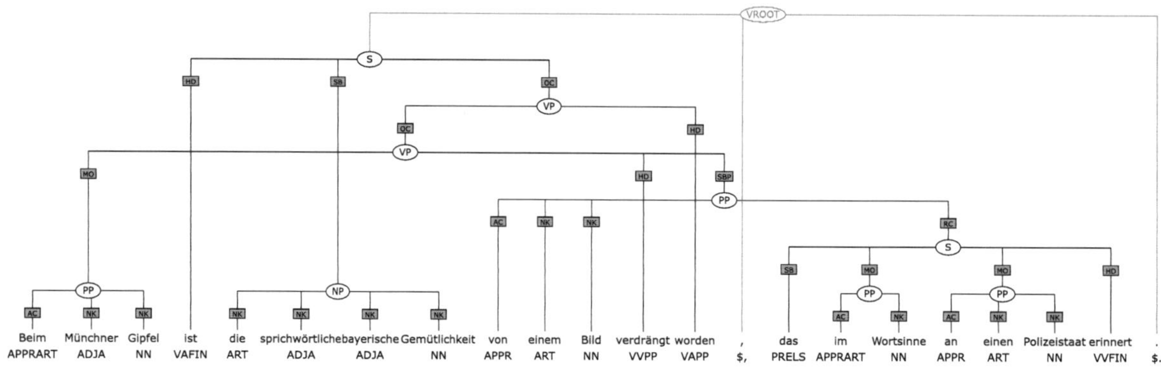

Figure 1: TIGER annotation with crossing branches.

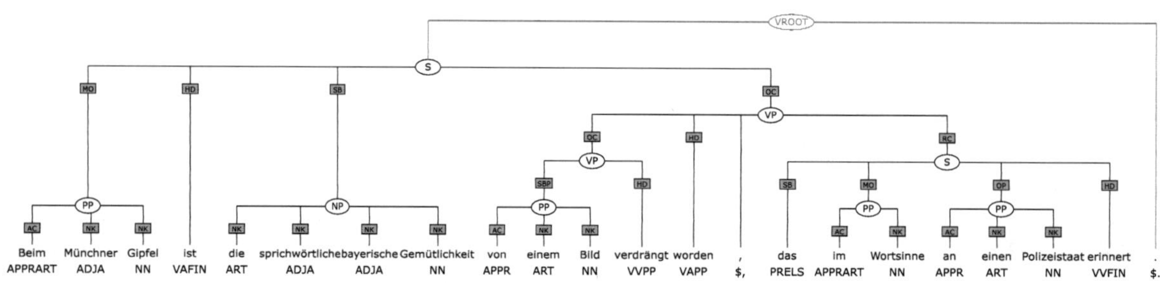

Figure 2: TIGER annotation with resolved crossing branches.

clude others, e.g. *RE* (repeated element) or *RC* (relative clause).

(7) Beim Münchner Gipfel ist die
At the Munich Summit is the
sprichwörtliche bayerische Gemütlichkeit
proverbial Bavarian 'Gemütlichkeit'
von einem Bild verdrängt worden, das
by a picture supplanted been, which
im Wortsinne an einen Polizeistaat
in the literal sense of a police state
erinnert.
reminds

'At the Munich Summit, the proverbial Bavarian 'Gemütlichkeit' was supplanted by an image that is evocative of a police state.'

Figure 1 shows a typical tree from the TIGER treebank for sentence (7). The syntactic categories are shown in circular nodes, the grammatical functions as edge labels in square boxes. A major phrasal category that serves to structure the sentence as a whole is the verb phrase (VP). It contains non-finite verbs (here: *verdrängt worden*) as well as their complements and adjuncts. The subject NP (*die sprichwörtliche bayerische Gemütlichkeit*) is outside the VP and, depending on its linear position, leads to crossing branches with the VP. This happens in all cases where the subject follows the finite verb as in Figure 1. Notice also that the PPs are completely flat. An additional crossing branch results from the direct attachment of the extraposed relative clause (the lower S node with function RC) to the noun that it modifies.

As mentioned in the previous section, TIGER trees must be transformed into trees without crossing branches prior to training PCFG parsers. The standard approach for this transformation is to re-attach crossing non-head constituents as sisters of the lowest mother node that dominates all the crossing constituent and its sister nodes in the original TIGER tree. Figure 2 shows the result of this transformation

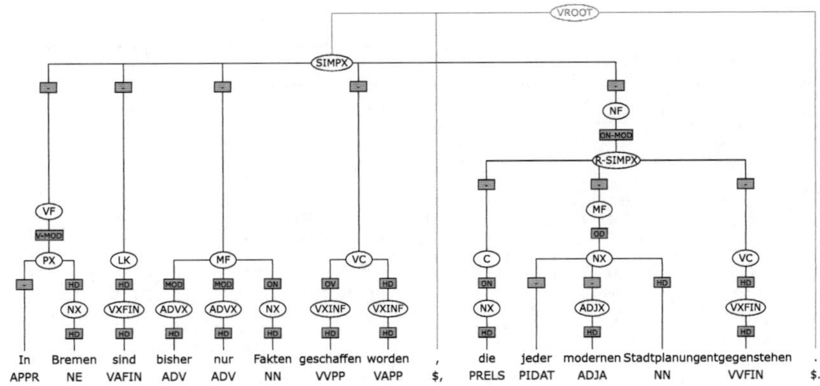

Figure 3: TüBa-D/Z annotation without crossing branches.

of the tree in Figure 1. Crossing branches not only arise with respect to the subject at the sentence level but also in cases of extraposition and fronting of partial constituents. As a result, approximately 30% of all TIGER trees contain at least one crossing branch. Thus, tree transformations have a major impact on the type of constituent structures that are used for training probabilistic parsing models.

Figure 3 shows the TüBa-D/Z annotation for sentence (8), a sentence with a very similar structure to the TIGER sentence shown in Figure 1. Crossing branches are avoided by the introduction of topological structures (here: VF, LK, MF, VC, NF, and C) into the tree. Notice also that compared to the TIGER annotation, TüBa-D/Z introduces more internal structure into NPs and PPs. In TüBa-D/Z, long-distance relationships are represented by a pure tree structure and specific functional labels. Thus, the extraposed relative clause is attached to the matrix clause directly, but its functional label *ON-MOD* explicates that it modifies the subject *ON*.

(8) In Bremen sind bisher nur Fakten geschaffen
In Bremen are so far only facts produced
worden, die jeder modernen Stadtplanung
been, which any modern city planning
entgegenstehen.
contradict

'In Bremen, so far only such attempts have been made that are opposed to any modern city planning.'

4.2 The Dependency Data

The constituent representations from both treebanks were converted into dependencies. The conversion aimed at finding dependency representations for both treebanks that are as similar to each other as possible. Complete identity is impossible because the treebanks contain different levels of distinction for different phenomena. The conversion is based on the original formats of the treebanks including crossing branches. The target dependency format was defined based on the dependency grammar by Foth (2003). For the conversion, we used pre-existing dependency converters for TIGER trees (Daum et al., 2004) and for TüBa-D/Z trees (Versley, 2005). The dependency representations of the trees in Figures 1 and 3 are shown in Figures 4 and 5. Note that the long-distance relationships are converted into non-projective dependencies.

5 Submissions and Results

The shared task drew submissions from 3 groups: the Berkeley group, the Stanford group, and the Växjö group. Four more groups or individuals had registered but did not submit any data. The submitted systems and results are described in detail in papers in this volume (Petrov and Klein, 2008; Rafferty and Manning, 2008; Hall and Nivre, 2008). All three systems submitted results for the constituent task. For the dependency task, the Växjö group had the only submission. For this reason, we will concentrate on the analysis of the constituent results and will mention the dependency results only shortly.

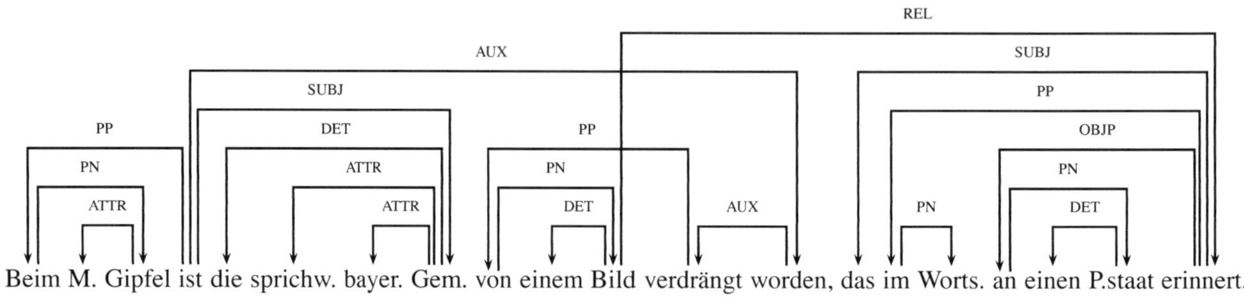

Figure 4: TIGER dependency annotation.

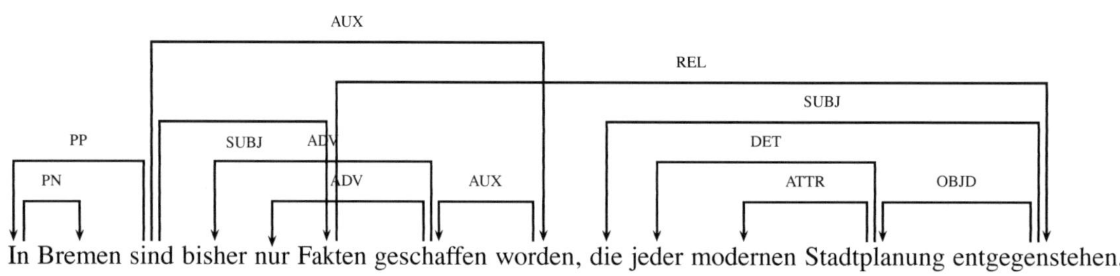

Figure 5: TüBa-D/Z dependency annotation.

5.1 Constituent Evaluation

The results of the constituent analysis are shown in Table 1. The evaluation was performed with regard to labels consisting of a combination of syntactic labels and grammatical functions. A subject noun phrase, for example, is only counted as correct if it has the correct yield, the correct label (i.e. *NP* for TIGER and *NX* for TüBa-D/Z), and the correct grammatical function (i.e. *SB* for TIGER and *ON* for TüBa-D/Z). The results show that the Berkeley parser reaches the best results for both treebanks. The other two parsers compete for second place. For TIGER, the Växjö parser outperforms the Stanford parser, but for TüBa-D/Z, the situation is reversed. This gives an indication that the Växjö parser seems better suited for the flat annotations in TIGER while the Stanford parser is better suited for the more hierarchical structure in TüBa-D/Z. Note that all parsers reach much higher F-scores for TüBa-D/Z.

A comparison of how well suited two different annotation schemes are for parsing is a surprisingly difficult task. A first approach would be to compare the parser performance for specific categories, such as for noun phrases, etc. However, this is not possible for TIGER and TüBa-D/Z. On the one hand, the range of phenomena described as noun phrases, for example, is different in the two treebanks. The most obvious difference in annotation schemes is that TüBa-D/Z annotates unary branching structures while TIGER does not. As a consequence, in TüBa-D/Z, all pronouns and substituting demonstratives are annotated as noun phrases; in TIGER, they are attached directly to the next higher node (cf. the relative pronouns, POS tag PRELS, in Figures 1 and 3). Kübler (2005) and Maier (2006) suggest a method for comparing such different annotation schemes by approximating them stepwise so that the decisions which result in major changes can be isolated. They come to the conclusion that the differences between the two annotation schemes is a least partially due to inconsistencies introduced into TIGER style annotations during the resolution of crossing branches. However, even this method cannot give any indication which annotation scheme provides more useful information for systems that use such parses as input. To answer this question, an *in vivo* evaluation would be necessary. It is, however, rather difficult to find systems into which a parser can be plugged in without too many modifications of the system.

On the other hand, it is a well-known fact that

system	TIGER			TüBa-D/Z		
	precision	recall	F-score	precision	recall	F-score
Berkeley	69.23	70.41	69.81	83.91	84.04	83.97
Stanford	58.52	57.63	58.07	79.26	79.22	79.24
Växjö	67.06	63.40	65.18	76.44	74.79	75.60

Table 1: The results of the constituent parsing task.

system	GF	TIGER			TüBa-D/Z		
		precision	recall	F-score	precision	recall	F-score
Berkeley	SB/ON	74.46	78.31	76.34	78.33	77.08	77.70
	OA	60.08	66.61	63.18	58.11	65.81	61.72
	DA/OD	49.28	41.72	43.19	59.46	44.72	51.05
Stanford	SB/ON	64.40	63.11	63.75	71.16	77.76	74.31
	OA	45.52	45.91	45.71	47.23	51.28	49.17
	DA/OD	12.40	9.82	10.96	24.42	8.54	12.65
Växjö	SB/ON	75.33	73.00	74.15	72.37	69.53	70.92
	OA	57.01	57.65	57.33	58.07	57.55	57.81
	DA/OD	55.45	37.42	44.68	63.75	20.73	31.29

Table 2: The results for subjects, accusative objects, and dative objects.

the PARSEVAL measures favor annotation schemes with hierarchical structures, such as in TüBa-D/Z, in comparison to annotation schemes with flat structures (Rehbein and van Genabith, 2007). Here, TIGER and TüBa-D/Z differ significantly: in TIGER, phrases receive a flat annotation. Prepositional phrases, for example, do not contain an explicitly annotated noun phrase. TüBa-D/Z phrases, in contrast, are more hierarchical; preposition phrases do contain a noun phrase, and non phrases distinguish between pre- and post-modification. For this reason, the evaluation presented in Table 1 must be taken with more than a grain of salt as a comparison of annotation schemes. However, it seems safe to follow Kübler et al. (Kübler et al., 2006) in the assumption that the major grammatical functions, subject (*SB/ON*), accusative object (*OA*), and dative object (*DA/OD*) are comparable. Again, this is not completely true because in the case of one-word NPs, these functions are attached to the POS tags and thus are given in the input. Another solution, which was pursued by Rehbein and van Genabith (2007), is the introduction of new unary branching nodes in the tree in cases where such grammatical functions are originally attached to the POS tag. We refrained from using this solution because it introduces further inconsistencies (only a subset of unary branching nodes are explicitly annotated), which make it difficult for a parser to decide whether to group such phrases or not. The evaluation shown in Table 2 is based on all nodes which were annotated with the grammatical function in question.

The results presented in Table 2 show that the differences between the two treebanks are inconclusive. While the Stanford parser performs consistently better on TüBa-D/Z, the Berkeley parser handles accusative objects better in TIGER, and the Växjö parser subjects and dative objects. The results indicate that the Berkeley parser profits from the TIGER annotation of accusative objects, which are grouped in the verb phrase while TüBa-D/Z groups all objects in their fields directly without resorting to a verb phrase. However, this does not explain why the Berkeley parser cannot profit from the subject attachment on the clause level in TIGER to the same degree.

5.2 Dependency Evaluation

The results of the dependency evaluation for the Växjö system are shown in Table 3. The results are

	TIGER		TüBa-D/Z	
UAS	92.63		91.45	
LAS	90.80		88.64	
	precision	recall	precision	recall
SUBJ	90.20	89.82	88.99	88.55
OBJA	77.93	82.19	77.18	82.71
OBJD	57.00	44.02	67.88	45.90

Table 3: The results of the dependency evaluation.

important for the comparison of constituent and dependency parsing since in the conversion to dependencies, most of the differences between the annotation schemes, and as a consequence, the preference of the PARSEVAL measures have been neutralized. Therefore, it is interesting to see that the results for TIGER are slightly better than the results for TüBa-D/Z, both for unlabeled (UAS) and labeled attachment scores. The reasons for these differences are unclear: either the TIGER texts are easier to parse, or the (original annotation and) conversion from TIGER is more consistent. Another surprising fact is that the dependency results are clearly better than the constituent ones. This is partly due to the fact that the dependency representation is often less informative than then constituent representation. One example for this can be found in coordinations: In dependency representations, the scope ambiguity in phrases like *young men and women* is not resolved. This gives parsers fewer opportunities to go wrong. However, this cannot explain all the differences. Especially the better performance on the major grammatical functions cannot be explained in this way.

A closer look at the grammatical functions shows that here, precision and recall are higher than for constituent parses. This is a first indication that dependency representation may be more appropriate for languages with freer word order. A comparison between the two treebanks is inconclusive: for the accusative object, the results are similar between the treebanks. For subjects, the results for TIGER are better while for dative objects, the results for TüBa-D/Z are better. This issue requires closer investigation.

6 Conclusion

This is the first shared task on parsing German, which provides training and test sets from both major treebanks for German, TIGER and TüBa-D/Z. For both treebanks, we provided a constituent and a dependency representation. It is our hope that these data sets will spark more interest in the comparison of different annotation schemes and their influence on parsing results. The evaluation of the three participating systems has shown that for both treebanks, the use of a latent variable grammar in the Berkeley system is beneficial. However, many questions remain unanswered and require further investigation: To what extent do the evaluation metrics distort the results? Does a measure exist that is neutral towards the differences in annotation? Is the dependency format better suited for parsing German? Are the differences between the dependency results of the two treebanks indicators that TIGER provides more important information for dependency parsing? Or can the differences be traced back to the conversion algorithms?

Acknowledgments

First and foremost, we want to thank all the people and organizations that generously provided us with treebank data and without whom the shared task would have been literally impossible: Erhard Hinrichs, University of Tübingen (TüBa-D/Z), and Hans Uszkoreit, Saarland University and DFKI (TIGER).

Secondly, we would like to thank Wolfgang Maier and Yannick Versley who performed the data conversions necessary for the shared task. Additionally, Wolfgang provided the scripts for the constituent evaluation.

References

Cristina Bosco, Vincenzo Lombardo, D. Vassallo, and Leonardo Lesmo. 2000. Building a treebank for Italian: a data-driven annotation scheme. In *Proceedings of the 2nd International Conference on Language Resources and Evaluation, LREC-2000*, Athens, Greece.

Sabine Brants, Stefanie Dipper, Silvia Hansen, Wolfgang Lezius, and George Smith. 2002. The TIGER treebank. In Erhard Hinrichs and Kiril Simov, editors, *Proceedings of the First Workshop on Treebanks and Linguistic Theories (TLT 2002)*, pages 24–41, Sozopol, Bulgaria.

Michael Daum, Kilian Foth, and Wolfgang Menzel. 2004. Automatic transformation of phrase treebanks to dependency trees. In *Proceedings of the 4th International Conference on Language Resources and Evaluation, LREC-2004*, Lisbon, Portugal.

Kilian Foth. 2003. Eine umfassende Dependenzgrammatik des Deutschen. Technical report, Fachbereich Informatik, Universität Hamburg.

Johan Hall and Joakim Nivre. 2008. A dependency-driven parser for German dependency and constituency representations. In *Proceedings of the ACL Workshop on Parsing German*, Columbus, OH.

Erhard Hinrichs, Sandra Kübler, Karin Naumann, Heike Telljohann, and Julia Trushkina. 2004. Recent developments in linguistic annotations of the TüBa-D/Z treebank. In *Proceedings of the Third Workshop on Treebanks and Linguistic Theories*, pages 51–62, Tübingen, Germany.

Sandra Kübler, Erhard W. Hinrichs, and Wolfgang Maier. 2006. Is it really that difficult to parse German? In *Proceedings of the 2006 Conference on Empirical Methods in Natural Language Processing, EMNLP 2006*, pages 111–119, Sydney, Australia.

Sandra Kübler. 2005. How do treebank annotation schemes influence parsing results? Or how not to compare apples and oranges. In *Proceedings of the International Conference on Recent Advances in Natural Language Processing, RANLP 2005*, pages 293–300, Borovets, Bulgaria.

Wolfgang Maier. 2006. Annotation schemes and their influence on parsing results. In *Proceedings of the ACL-2006 Student Research Workshop*, Sydney, Australia.

Mitchell Marcus, Beatrice Santorini, and Mary Ann Marcinkiewicz. 1993. Building a large annotated corpus of English: The Penn Treebank. *Computational Linguistics*, 19(2):313–330.

S. Montegmagni, F. Barsotti, M. Battista, N. Calzolari, O. Corazzari, A. Zampolli, F. Fanciulli, M. Massetani, R. Raffaelli, R. Basili, M. T. Pazienza, D. Saracino, F. Zanzotto, N. Mana, F. Pianesi, and R. Delmonte. 2000. The Italian syntactic-semantic treebank: Architecture, annotation, tools and evaluation. In *Proceedings of the Workshop on Linguistically Interpreted Corpora LINC-2000*, pages 18–27, Luxembourg.

Joakim Nivre, Johan Hall, Sandra Kübler, Ryan McDonald, Jens Nilsson, Sebastian Riedel, and Deniz Yuret. 2007. The CoNLL 2007 shared task on dependency parsing. In *Proceedings of the CoNLL 2007 Shared Task. Joint Conference on Empirical Methods in Natural Language Processing and Computational Natural Language Learning, EMNLP-CoNLL 2007*, Prague, Czech Republic.

Slav Petrov and Dan Klein. 2008. Parsing German with language agnostic latent variable grammars. In *Proceedings of the ACL Workshop on Parsing German*, Columbus, OH.

Anna Rafferty and Christopher Manning. 2008. Parsing three German treebanks: Lexicalized and unlexicalized baselines. In *Proceedings of the ACL Workshop on Parsing German*, Columbus, OH.

Ines Rehbein and Josef van Genabith. 2007. Treebank annotation schemes and parser evaluation for German. In *Proceedings of the 2007 Joint Conference on Empirical Methods in Natural Language Processing and Computational Natural Language Learning, EMNLP-CoNLL*, pages 630–639, Prague, Czech Republic.

Geoffrey Sampson. 1993. The SUSANNE corpus. *ICAME Journal*, 17:125 – 127.

Wojciech Skut, Thorsten Brants, Brigitte Krenn, and Hans Uszkoreit. 1998. A linguistically interpreted corpus of German newspaper texts. In *ESSLLI Workshop on Recent Advances in Corpus Annotation*, Saarbrücken, Germany.

Heike Telljohann, Erhard W. Hinrichs, Sandra Kübler, and Heike Zinsmeister, 2006. *Stylebook for the Tübingen Treebank of Written German (TüBa-D/Z)*. Seminar für Sprachwissenschaft, Universität Tübingen, Germany.

Christine Thielen and Anne Schiller. 1994. Ein kleines und erweitertes Tagset fürs Deutsche. In Helmut Feldweg and Erhard Hinrichs, editors, *Lexikon & Text*, pages 215–226. Niemeyer, Tübingen.

Yannick Versley. 2005. Parser evaluation across text types. In *Proceedings of the Fourth Workshop on Treebanks and Linguistic Theories, TLT 2005*, pages 209–220, Barcelona, Spain.

Sean Wallis and Gerald Nelson. 2006. The British component of the International Corpus of English. Release 2. CD-ROM. London: Survey of English Usage, UCL.

Author Index